WHAT'S IN A NAME?
— Richard Siegal

Among other things, The Bakery is a business. But as an arts organization it is, by definition, a business whose economic identity should be subject to a critical, artistic gaze. I wonder at the significance in conflating the opposing social forces of art and money, of housing them under one intention. How is the artistic impulse made to behave as market-ready? How can the manner in which we compete for resources coexist with our inchoate need to create? What is the source of our value? These questions appear particularly salient in our restive search to identify the contemporary.

In reflecting on the act of launching a business in the deregulated Noughties, the apogee of corporate power, my choice of brand names now strikes me as ironically appropriate. I recall drawing up lists of homely locations in emulation of the New York venues I frequented in my East Village days: The Kitchen, The Livingroom, The Knitting Factory, etc. The most congenial among them seemed to have been spoken for. "The Bakery," however, had yet to be optioned as a .org domain, remarkable for 2005 when virtual territory was still finite and largely colonized. "Bakery" struck the tone, was viscerally inviting, and had the additional advantage of being a highly recognizable word for non-native English speakers. This last attribute was a particularly important brand asset for my aspiring multi-national corporation, of which I was the only employee.

Although my bargain with Capitalism has always been specious, I was nonetheless still apt to view multinationals as heroic in the following respect: their ubiquity was admirable. Though their means did not justify their every end, they did manage to defy time and space. Pirates, really, operating in global waters that are legally gray. They were freer than I was and could act with deregulated impunity. Their immaterial bodies were impervious to the ravages of time and use. These were gods made in our own image. In blatant imitation, I conceptualized The Bakery as a global brand, without locus, an idea to be affixed to any activity in which I was involved; paramount freedom equated with unbridled choice. I wanted to assume the agency of Capitalism. Framed thusly, founding a company was itself a durational, critical gesture interrogating the organization of society in the Information Age.

These were also the rising tide years of Facebook, of reality TV, flashmobs, and webcams streaming 24/7. Napster and YouTube opened an emancipating window on the autocrats of culture. Crowd culture was coming of age. As prophesied by Coppola in *Hearts of*

Darkness: A Filmmaker's Apocalypse, technological accessibility was leveling the playing field. But as an individual *performing* artist I was straddling the old and new economies. I could not work from home because my understanding of performance denotes itinerancy, a seeking out of the complexity of crowds in real time and shared space. Most of us are still minstrels. There was nothing to do but to put myself into motion. I waded into a globally diffused, culture economy. My frequent flyer account soared and I availed myself of all the time and space-flattening technology the market had recently brought within reach of the consumer. Soon my lifestyle approached a reflection of the corporate entities that achieve creative power by shedding their own bodies. For a dancer, this was a paradox to aspire to. The Bakery (dare I say any dance company?) is a quixotic attempt to institutionalize the body. My attitude anyhow remains radically optimistic.

Now for the irony: A bakery is an anachronistic space, paradigmatic of precisely those notions of community most susceptible to the crucible of globalization. "Bakery" intentionally elicits artisanal expertise, physical address and, moreover, neighborhood—all facets of community decidedly on the retreat. Nonetheless The Bakery was also conceived of as a global brand. I had co-opted the prerogative we have granted our capitalist champions to assume contradiction. In melding the antitheses into one name (indeed we operated for a time under the name The Bakery Paris Berlin NYC), our "glocal" company became an artistic gesture expressing the aspect of the contemporary condition that is about living the dilemma of freedom *versus* contentment. In an age of low-cost airlines and VOIP, Shengen agreements and trading blocs, unlimited communication and mobility give the impression of freedom, a return to our nomadic natures, the irrelevance of national identity. And yet, having so rapidly diluted our cultural inheritance we are left with a liminal identity. At best we are members of a community we cannot yet perceive, much less name. The nature and quality of social intercourse has been dislocated. The Bakery was a tongue-in-cheek standard around which I proposed we rally.

One project The Bakery has since undertaken was to document and analyze five years of work based on the If/Then Methodology. The DVD booklet, *If/Then Dialogues*, defines by example this artistic attitude. If/Then Methodology is a game-based, syntactical, and notational system. As a choreographic approach it began with the duet, *If/Then* (2005). The tactic is to allow the practitioner to inscribe causal relationships between events of varying predictability. If/Then is concerned with the order of things, but not the nature of them. It is ambivalent toward conventions and classes of ideas. Rather, it is predicated on indifferentia and the primacy of choice. It is a randomizer of input that assumes the validity of Whatever, contenting itself by simply enacting communication. A participant's agency is elicited in proportion to their idiosyncrasies and ability to cooperate within the system. To date, this is best expressed in the performances *Stranger* (2004) and *Civic Mimic* (2011). When performed by large numbers, the dynamic tendencies of groups are fostered: *©oPirates* (2010), *Critical Gaze* (2010), *Logic Gate* (2010), *Set of All Sets* (2010). As If/Then is fundamentally dialectical and content is immaterial, cross-disciplinarity and collectivity are implicit. All branches of knowledge are potentially constructive. The working method is articulated in ever finer detail with each artistic process: performance, publication, installation, public talk, workshop, and website. *If/Then Dialogues* attests to a lively cross-disciplinary engagement from a growing community, who collaborate under the name The Bakery.

Today, seven years since The Bakery's inception, the local is a concept in retreat, consigned to a defensive posture among consumer activists. Multinationals have been slapped on the wrist but continue to radiate inevitability. We are bearing witness to the coming of a new world order, yet to arrive. Until then, indistinction is the order of the day. Our paradigm is incertitude and I am motivated to describe the experience, to embrace the ambiguity. The Bakery was floated on precisely such vagaries.

By neither renouncing the market nor aligning ourselves with it, a diffused and highly flexible arts organization has been created. Our approach sources radical tendencies and yet, for example, is sustained by government grants and state-funded institutions, demonstrating its pertinence to the status quo. We are nurtured by the tension between the opposing positions of cultural production, change, and conservation. The contradiction is especially fascinating when it is the source of artistic productivity.

The coordinative principle of If/Then, which expresses choice, multiplicity, collective responsibility, and decentralization, extends to The Bakery as an organization. In this sense, the origins and meaning of both the work and the way of working can be found in the conflation of cultural and economic conditions specific to our present. Companies like ours could not have gained currency nor perhaps even been conceived of in an era other than our own. Is The Bakery the new normal? Its ethos is so closely aligned with the present that it arguably produces, and is, an artwork radically demonstrative of the idea of the contemporary itself. The Bakery is an idea in action meant to define our ineffable, unbrandable moment.

This book is an effort to inductively describe The Bakery. Each of the essays serves to draw the reader's attention to a concern that motivates me as an artist. Collectively they circumscribe and name the commonality. I wholeheartedly thank all the contributors for lending their expertise in the endeavor. The results are evident.

RICHARD SIEGAL

Founder and artistic director of The Bakery. Recognized by a New York Dance and Performance Bessie Award, The German National Theatre "Faust" Award, a Beaumarchais-SACD Award, and The Mouson Award, Richard Siegal has generated international attention for a body of work that includes performances, new media projects, workshops, and publications.

He has been commissioned by festivals and venues including Festival d'Automne, Rencontres Chorégraphiques, Ircam, Centre Pompidou, YCAM, Tanz im August, Ballett Frankfurt, Danspace/NYC, and Théâtre National de Chaillot.

His work with live musicians has led him to collaborate with Alberto Posadas (*Glossopoeia*), Diane Labrosse (*Double Story*), Lorenzo Bianchi (*©oPirates* and *Homo Ludens*), Eric-Maria Couturier (*Opus Infinity* and *Homo Ludens*), Wolfgang Zamastil (*Homo Ludens* and *As If Stranger*), Arto Lindsay (*Muscle*) and Hubert Machnik (*Civic Mimic*).

Collaborations with architects and architectural designers include work with François Roche (*Civic Mimic*), Virginie Mira (*Stranger Trilogy* and *Glossopoeia*), Peter Zuspan (*Multinatural (blackout)* and *Muscle*) and Alexander Kada (Venice Biennale of Architecture).

Richard Siegal has been artist/choreographer-in-residence at ZKM/Karlsruhe, Bennington College and The Baryshnikov Arts Center. As a faculty member of the American Dance Festival, he curated the annual Forsythe Festival. Siegal is a MacDowell fellow and honorary member of The Bolshoi Ballet's "Benoit de la Danse."

In conjunction with debates about choreographic approaches, the art world has experienced a drift from products geared to the market and institutional requirements to process-oriented, multi-annual or performative models. Today, collaborative and interdisciplinary working methods in choreography keep challenging the idea of the institution —structurally, politically, aesthetically and socially—at the same time offering access to an ongoing thinking process regarding the transformation and emergence of new artistic and cultural forms.

In this context, *Richard Siegal*'s network for interdisciplinary research and production, The Bakery, plans to open new avenues of discourse, unlock new possibilities for artistic dialogue by permanently confronting various ways of thinking and working in the field of the arts, whilst capitalizing on existing institutions and resources. With its hybridity of works for different artistic and social contexts—dance centers and festivals, museums and art biennials—The Bakery seeks to surpass expectations based on standardized modes of representation by inciting co-responsibility or, in the words of French philosopher and educationalist Jacques Rancière, by the "blurring of the boundary between those who act and those who look."[1]

Two of The Bakery's recent works —*©oPirates* (2010) and *Civic Mimic* (2011)—are preoccupied with questions of spectatorship, modes of production, and community. Both artistic works are open and receptive to the participation of the public. They propose idealized, temporary communities in a shared and complex environment. *©oPirates*, through its function as a relational piece, creates a kind of self-organizing community composed of the public mixed together with pre-existing local groups—rollerbladers, folk dancers, political activists, and choir members along with parkour enthusiasts. The professional dancers of The Bakery are both on stage and in the public, transforming the shape and content of the piece with each and every performance.

©oPirates highlights the relationship between spectator and performer within a set of defined and non-defined boundaries. Within the space of action, shared by ticket holders and performers, we find the boundaries blurred between those observing and those being observed. This work is inspired by the idea of "the coming community," as formulated by Italian philosopher Giorgio Agamben in his book of the same title.[2] He argues that community is constituted by sharing ideas and sharing affinities, fueled by the desire and the need to grow and learn. The transmission of ideas or knowledge, according to Agamben, is at the heart of the communal being, driving community as much as it drives singularities. Knowledge is what differentiates one individual from another, which can be shared in the presence of others. Contrary to traditional modes of exploring modalities of collective being (i.e. philosophy, sociology, politics), *©oPirates* explores community through modes of performance.

The investigation elicits many questions, including some of the following: How does the body inhabit community? How does the individual body relate to the body politic? What particular language(s) does the body produce when one comes into contact with the other? What provokes their coming together? What are the limits, the borders of sharing? How can one be oneself and share at the same time? The piece sought to examine and redefine these questions as they unfold throughout the work in its various sequences.[3]

The queries raised in *©oPirates* led to further research for The Bakery's most recent project, *Civic Mimic*. Choosing such a title combined two major philosophical aims. One was to reflect on the civic practices of imagination in a public space. The other was to reflect on the longstanding discourse on imitation and ownership. Motivated by the observation of forms of embodiment and representation, *Civic Mimic* seemed capable of reformulating the conditions of belonging and exclusion, order and spontaneity, routine and chance into a spectacle of "social choreography."

As social choreography *Civic Mimic* investigates the notion and potentials of temporary communities. Going beyond a conventional staging, the production situates the body at the intersection between the individual and the collective. It incorporates bodies in their social relationships, frustrating the division between spectator and performer in a conditional, transactional space. The concept takes into consideration Homi K. Bhaba's demand that we transform our understanding of cross-cultural relations in order to produce a new form of cultural awareness and critical self-understanding.[4]

The Paris-based architectural office R&Sie(n) was invited to collaborate, based on Siegal's ongoing research into performative architecture and his dialogue with designers, architects, and media artists. François Roche's thirty-five meter, white architectural structure—part stage, part kinetic sculpture—blurs the classical division between stage (space of action) and auditorium (space of contemplation). By creating an architecture of incertitude and instability he determines the spatial and physical experience of both performers and spectators and thus triggers changes in the crowd dynamics.

Linked to the research regarding civic practices of imagination in public was a second objective; to reflect upon the longstanding discourse on imitation and ownership, which has become a battlefield in today's debate on intellectual property. In his philosophical meditation *In Praise of Copying*,[5] Canadian author Marcus Boon discusses the hostility toward copying and seeks to show what is politically at stake in the way we view copying in the age of globalization.[6] Thus imitation, repetition and instant reconfiguration became some of the main structural elements for the dancers of *Civic Mimic*. These were defined originally by the choreographic strategy developed by Richard Siegal. His game-based If/Then Methodology, a syntactical and notational system, allows the movement material accumulated over the course of the rehearsals to be recomposed each time it is performed. The games are composed of simple gestures and rules that are very binary: *If you do x, then I do y or z*. Each game shares a common configuration, or "hub," which links it to other games. The results are non-linear performances with multiple structural itineraries and multiple conclusions requiring intellectually and physically mature performers. The dancers of *Civic Mimic* are, moreover, faced with a further variable: a heterogenous audience who share the space equally. The spectators, either in flux or static, either acting or looking, inspire patterns of physical behavior which challenge the six dancers in their decision-making.

The music, too, correlates with the choreographic process of gameplay. *Hubert Machnik*, *Civic Mimic*'s seventh performer, locates himself between his own composition and the spatial/temporal decisions of the dancers. Within the interdependent systems of crowds, material, and gestures, the performers thematize not only the act of choice in dance and music, but also negotiate the resulting unpredictable reciprocity.[7]

Civic Mimic has so far experienced different versions due to the unpredictablity of audiences, the real-time dialogue of the performers, as well as the changing venues: from white cube (Festspielhaus Hellerau, Dresden) to black box (Muffathalle, Munich; Tafelhalle, Nuremberg) and beyond that to public foyer (Théâtre National de Chaillot, Paris). The constant oscillation between actor and spectator is amplified by an additional, social layer. *Civic Mimic* generates a hybrid audience through the integration of a great number of volunteers as co-actors, whom Siegal leads beforehand in workshops. Through their agency the spectator is tacitly invited to abandon convention and become an actor.

The singular potential of volunteering in a social choreography points to civic processes based on a shared practice of imagination. *Civic Mimic* is difficult to categorize. It can be called many things: a dance performance, a performance installation, a social choreography, an event, a spectacle, or happening. Whatever the name, it relies entirely upon dialogical alertness and therefore might be best termed a conversation.

In the long run, The Bakery's goal is to create decelerated, hassle-free work environments in which processes are made transparent, ideas are cross-linked, and artistic gestures are made subject to both reflection and criticism for performers and spectators alike. The Bakery feels it is critical to establish a wider forum developing a long-term, content-oriented agenda. Its mission is to sustain diverse partneships whilst assessing the socio-cultural and aesthetic impact of the productions.

Author, theater director and visual artist *Tim Etchells* approaches the concept of performance by a virtuosic assembling of observations, finds, stories, and notes. By critically questioning historical positions and shaping new definitions the text mirrors his innovative, cross-disciplinary artistic practice throughout the last thirty years.

In his fictional narrative on the construction of memory, architect *Didier Faustino* describes the journey of his protagonist Branko, neither an architect nor an artist but a modern flâneur, who traces the residues of a forgotten past in abandoned rooms and buildings integrating all his senses. This poetic approach is underpinned by a text in which Faustino reveals his notion of a permeable, "performative architecture of doubt," perceived through the body and the senses.

The witty and expressive essay by philosopher *Barbara Formis*, co-dramaturge of *©oPirates*, traces her experiences of the performance from various points of view, relating the multi-layered nature of her role—as spectator, philosopher, dramaturge, and performer.

Founder and curator of the New York biennial PERFORMA, *RoseLee Goldberg* shares a behind-the-scenes account of the highly professional politics of festival-making. By inventing new strategies for crossing disciplinary and institutional boundaries she demonstrates the value of flexibility in today's contemporary performance world.

In their dialogue, composers *Hubert Machnik* and *Heiner Goebbels* discuss challenges and differences regarding their specific approaches to musical composition and enactment in live performance vis-à-vis their interpretation of space, variation, repetition, improvisation, and technology.

Situated between notation and open score, Machnik further dissects the process of writing music, of inventing and programming a specific musical instrument and his own performance in *Civic Mimic*.

By reflecting on the Arab Spring and the Occupy Movements as points of departure, *Chantal Pontbriand*, co-dramaturge of *©oPirates*, defines the tropes of performativity and ephemerality as quests for the experience and exploration of the unknown.

New Media artist and performance researcher *Chris Salter*'s contribution calls for the concept of performance to be reclaimed and invigorated by the new fields that feed it, creating a more expanded definition encompassing all forms of life.

Seen from the vantage point of long-term research dancer-choreographer *Susan Sgorbati*'s essay on Emergent Improvisation responds to questions regarding choreographic practice today as an innovative, complex, and interconnected process.

1 Jacques Rancière, *The Emancipated Spectator*, translated by Gregory Elliott (London: Verso, 2011), page 19.

2 Giorgio Agamben, *The Coming Community*, translated by Michael Hardt (Minneapolis, MN: University of Minnesota Press, 1993).

3 See also the essays of Barbara Formis and Chantal Pontbriand.

4 Homi K. Bhaba, *The Location of Culture* (London; New York: Routledge, 1994).

5 Marcus Boon, *In Praise of Copying* (Cambridge, MA: Harvard University Press, 2010).

6 Ibid., pages 245–248.

7 See also Hubert Machnik's essay on composing for *Civic Mimic*.

We would like to thank all contributing authors for their thoughtful and inspiring contributions, and our special thanks go to RoseLee Goldberg for providing our book title. We would also like to thank our financial supporters: Kulturstiftung des Bundes, Kulturreferat der Landeshauptstadt Munich, and Muffathalle, Munich for making this book possible. Our deepest respect goes to the team at Spector Books who have understood our endeavors from the outset. Our personal thanks go to all members of The Bakery.

CHRISTINE PETERS

From 1992 to 1998 she was Project Director and from 1998 to 2003 Artistic Director at Künstlerhaus Mousonturm, Frankfurt am Main. Her main focus is the interdisciplinary production of theory and practice in contemporary art. Since 2004 she has worked as a freelance curator, e.g. for Theater der Welt 2005, Stuttgart, the steirischer herbst festival Graz, 2006 (here she co-curated the group exhibition *Protections* at Kunsthaus Graz), and Richard Siegal/The Bakery (since 2006). From 2008 to 2009 she was artistic consultant for Tanzplan Deutschland's initiative *Dance/Curating between Theory and Practice* (Berlin, Leipzig, Hamburg). Since 2005 she has taught "Curating in the Interdisciplinary Context" at various universities and academies. In 2010 she curated the preview lecture, essay, and performance series *Schöne Aussicht* for the Theater der Welt festival in Essen and Mülheim and co-curated the group exhibition *Play Admont* at the Museum for Contemporary Art in Admont, Austria. She co-curated the interdisciplinary conference "Beyond Curating" at PACT Zollverein Essen, 2011. She was Artistic Director of the temporary art space "Globe" at the Deutsche Bank Towers in Frankfurt am Main in 2010–11 and is co-curator of the group exhibition *Acts of Voicing* at the Württembergischer Kunstverein Stuttgart, October 2012.

DIETA SIXT

She has had a longstanding career with the Goethe-Institut, with directorships in Montreal, Washington, San Francisco, and New York, as well as in Europe. Her academic background includes a doctorate in cultural policy from the University of Hamburg, an MA in German Language and Literature, and an MA in Linguistics. Her expertise in arts management covers numerous international projects and publications in the areas of dance, theater, media arts, film, and cultural studies. She currently divides her time between activities as a freelance cultural curator and Executive Director of The Bakery. She is an accredited foreign correspondent of the Foreign Press Association New York.

THE PIRACY OF THE SENSIBLE[1]

On ©o*Pirates* (2010), a work by Richard Siegal

— Barbara Formis

THE SPECTATOR

I

THE PERFORMER

II

THE DRAMATURGE

III

THE PHILOSOPHER

IV

I

I queue up at the entrance to the theatre. It's cold, I haven't got the right coat on and I'm alone in the middle of a mass of people. It's the premiere. The public crowd around, mingle, and look at each other. Hands are shaken, kisses are swapped and smiles are aimed at suitable addressees. The human exchange is moderately warm. I recognize a few faces, people I've met but whose names I've forgotten and so I dodge them to avoid awkward conversation. There is some excitement in the air: it's the premiere but also people in the dance world are expecting something from *©oPirates*. It's been announced as a show which is not a show, a dance celebration inviting participation, a massive choreographic enterprise tying together amateur groups, singers and acrobats—it's unheard of, it's new, and it's very cold in the queue. Why aren't the doors opening? I start to get impatient: enough of these events that frustrate the spectators just to produce a sensation, making us stand for hours, making us wait when there's nothing to wait for ... ah, now the doors open, as long as this blond in fake fur doesn't push in. That's right sweetcups, I was first and you can back up. I show my ticket and the nice usher tells me I get a free drink. Now that's what I like. Something new—the spectators are given something to drink. An easy gesture, but not so bad.

The venue is enormous, an empty unfinished place with six metre high ceilings. There's lounge music and soft lighting, a DJ box on a platform and a very long bar serving beer and cocktails. The entrance is surrounded by a giant white curtain used for video projections. The public push eagerly towards the bar, giving each other a few discreet and well timed elbows. I almost feel like boycotting the bar. Do I have to be trampled to get my free beer? Forget it, or forget it for now, I'll come back later. Except it's getting hotter inside and I'm thirsty. Bother. Might as well try to get that beer. The music is

II

I queue up at the entrance to the theatre. It's cold. I forgot to grab my coat when I left through the stage door. I was given a ticket I didn't pay for: a fake so it looks right, so I'm really one of the public. God it's cold. I hope I don't have to wait that long. It's the premiere. The public crowd around, mingle and look at each other. Hands are shaken, kisses are swapped and smiles are aimed at suitable addressees. I pretend to be alone in the middle of people. I see other performers a few metres away but I pretend not to know them. We mix with the public, incognito. Once we're inside we'll have to adapt to the strange situation of being performers without a stage, blended into the audience, at ground level, in the midst of this corporeal mass formed by spectators. It's the premiere and I've got butterflies. But I can't show it, nor can I do my ritual relaxation exercises. I have to deal with the nerves without people around me noticing.

Finally the doors open. For a second I almost feel like I actually am a spectator, someone who has just come to see a show. In a way this isn't entirely wrong, because I too will depend on the chance reactions of the crowd and the interactions that occur, and the spectators, in any case, will be less passive than in the normal theatrical format. The performers will be less on show and the spectators will act more—with the hope they'll meet somewhere in the middle. I hand over my ticket and take the stub for a free drink and immediately head to the bar to use it. The barman knows me, winks and fills my glass to the top; it's to wish me luck. It's not going to be easy managing all of the different scores we've learnt in the middle of all these people, making a space for oneself, connecting with people, getting the atmosphere going and especially managing to see the other performers who are part of my group. We have never been able to rehearse in this kind of context with 250 extra people in the space. We spoke

III

I have to find a method. The groups are so different from each other. Amateurs of folk dances mixed with professionals from the world of contemporary dance; belly-dancers, a soprano, a church choir, acrobats. We're never going to pull it off: finding something common underneath these differences, finding gestures that can be communicated, passed from body to body; finding a way to create a "being-together" without destroying the differences, whilst conserving identities. And these identities are completely incompatible. Dialogue seems difficult to me, ineffective, lacking any logical reason for its existence.

Why should a flamenco dancer share his experience with a German IT specialist who doesn't even know how to tap his foot in time with the music? Why should a traditional Hungarian music chorist confront a young rebel from the parkour group, who climbs the walls of the city? Wouldn't it be better if each remained inside her or his own identity and culture, each confined to her or his sector or ghetto? Wouldn't it be better if there was no mixing? It'd certainly be simpler, each community staying in its corner; it'd be much simpler but it's impossible and inhuman. Besides, if you think about it, we desperately try to base the convenience of our societies on such an inhumane principle. This is what happens in our towns, our urban spaces, our streets, our public transport. Everyone for himself, to each his own. Lock the door. Don't look.

The value of this work, halfway between theatre, dance, song, the music hall and happening, lies precisely in the riskiness of its wager—putting together what doesn't go together easily, causing irritation, difficulty and distance: different cultures; incomparable corporeal possibilities; mutually incomprehensible languages; amateurs with professionals; pop music with opera; performers with spectators; structure with mess; choreography

IV

I feel alone in the middle of people and yet I live with them, in a direct syntonic rapport according to a continual relationship in which the other defines me. My solitude encounters other singularities in a mirror effect through which I see myself without really recognizing myself, in which I suppose there is an identitarian linearity or continuity without being able to either refute or prove such a hypothesis. "The coming being is a whatever being" is how Giorgio Agamben describes the contemporary communitarian entity; an amalgam of singularities without any specific features, lacking a unique identity, but gathered together in an "inessential community".[5]

This is precisely what *©oPirates* incorporates in the lived experience of the dance. *©oPirates* is the spectacle of our questions and aspirations, our dreams and desires, our generosity and our fears; a spectacle which becomes a festival and encourages the audience members to get up from their comfortable chairs in order to participate in the work and activate its meaning, its purpose. It's a spectacle which is not only "collective" but more specifically "communitarian". If the collective can be reduced to an assembly of individuals—as Sartre understood this term, according to a triple relation of "reciprocity", "separation" and "alterity"—the community, on the other hand, is a collective become an entity through the solidarity of a project.[6] This change in status occurs without destroying individual singularities or the solitude proper to each member of the community. Solitude does not arise from pure passivity because "solitude is a project" and there are always "solitary behaviours".[7] My identity becomes that of "whoever", precisely when I compare it to other subjectivities, to other solitudes, without trying to extract an archetype from it.

The community produced here is thus not based on a distribution of abilities organized good. But when is the show going to start? Some smoke pours out of a machine. The videos get a little more lively. The music is turned up. I look at the dark figures of spectators around me, or rather against me since there isn't a spare centimetre of free space. It's like being in a nightclub. That must be the idea. The music is turned up even more. Is that barman going to look my way? Hello, I'm here! Yes, one beer please. What? A beer thanks! Yes, from the tap. OK, thanks! You have to shout to make yourself heard. Perhaps I'd better be quiet and make the best of it—enjoy[2]!

Suddenly people start dancing to the music. Well, not me. I came to see the show, not to have fun. Groups start to form, semicircles of friends. I have the impression that someone is trying to pick me up. No, no, I'm just looking. OK, I'm also imperceptibly moving my head in time to the music. Very discreet. People start dancing in lines. Choreographed gestures emerge clumsily here and there. A few shouts are heard. And then suddenly some folkloric dancers carry out their ritual movements. Disco music blends with an accordion and then starts up again at full blast. Acrobats climb up the platform and perform death defying jumps. It all seems improvised and natural, like a festive whirlwind which takes shape almost in spite of us. Several circles are formed. I can't see everything, people are in front of me. I can only guess what's happening. I'm trying not to miss the show when I'm actually in it. An opera singer appears, standing on the bar. She is magnificent. The music stops and the only thing we hear is her soprano. Like an apparition. And then the disco rhythms take up again quietly underneath her voice and bear it up until she is absorbed by the beat. I hadn't noticed but the curtain has moved and the space has deepened, the video images are clearer. People turn naturally towards the screen. And then all of a sudden like an enormous liner sinking in the ocean a huge theatrical stage breaks through the screen as if on rollers—dancers jump onto it as it glides over the spectators' heads and they go crazy like at a rock concert.

The atmosphere is unbelievable. The public is exalted. The alcohol worked ... the show explodes. Violent raging punk songs; a vertiginous athletic choreography which smells of bodies, of sex. Carnal music, seduction, victory cries and dance struggles. The whirlwind continues in a spiral of women in traditional costumes, in full colourful skirts swirling around bearing bottles of water on their heads, arms stretched straight out to the sides like living about it, we imagined it and we even tried to simulate it by putting chairs and obstacles between us. But this is the very first time we've had to deal with the real thing: this is a premiere in every sense of the term. Whatever happens,we will never have rehearsed it and we'll never be able to reproduce it. Every performance will be entirely unique because everything depends on the number of spectators, on the kind of atmosphere created and on a million other details. I wonder what Nietzsche would have thought, the eternal return of difference ... the same protocols, the same scores, but bringing about a completely unpredictable event. This is an open work made up of gestures and bodies that nobody could master, model or plan. My beer is nice and cold, the music is good and up the top of the scaffolding I can just see the lighting and sound desks where Lorenzo, the composer, and Richard, the choreographer, are watching over the public's entrance. I would really like to be able to see like they can, to observe from above without being observed in turn. But I have to concentrate: I have to let myself be absorbed by the party atmosphere that is starting up without forgetting my instructions, the order of the show, and the performances by other participants in this spectacle now become a collective work. The music is turned up and it starts to get hotter. The stagehands close the doors and get into place. I look at my watch—it's almost time. I hear the cue for the start and I turn discreetly towards the place where the first performance is supposed to begin. Thank god I'm not in the first group. I note with sly pleasure that the audience haven't noticed anything yet. I suddenly feel powerful, alone in the midst of ignorance. Beginning is difficult. We're intimidated by the unknown, by the audience's reactions. A few clumsy gestures are made here and there. We try to find our place, try to carry out what we are supposed to do at the same time as connecting with the people around us. And then, here and there, the public start to react, and it's almost imperceptible. It's not clear they understand exactly what's happening but they're letting themselves go, they're joining in the movement, and they're sure of themselves, they've got astonishing confidence. I'm relieved but also a little disturbed by the intensity of what's happening. How can it be so easy for strangers to hold each other's hands, dance together, encourage each other, applaud and swap places to the rhythm of the music? It can't be the alcohol alone, because one glass is not enough for such joy. I'm amazed. And all with improvisation; writing with bodies; me with the other. Being together means a party and a war at the same time. This can imply a joy in which each inscribes their own singularity in a great spiral of words and gestures. This spiral cannot be smooth and linear but has to incorporate all the tensions and difficulties of collective work. The method of this "being-together" must present itself in an abrupt and inopportune manner; for it to represent plurality in unity it must bear within it a certain amount of illegality and abuse. This method cannot be anything other than "piracy", a method of indecent appropriation. Piracy allows the work to be composed in an unexpected and abnormal manner according to a ludic mechanism which is easy to use: I steal something from you, you steal something from me. I don't get to decide what you steal from me, I'm not going to be able to teach you what I'd like, but you decide to draw the lesson which seems to you to be the best adapted to your needs and demands. In becoming reciprocal thieves we learn to blur our differences. We enquire into the subtle lines between identity and difference and trespass the order established by communitarian discriminations. It's not a question of generosity, but a principle of survival. The status quo is transformed: legitimacy is created through sabotage; that is the principle of piracy. Collective piracy, the legalization of theft, allows a community to be founded on abduction, on co-piracy. *©oPirates* is neither a simple performance nor uniquely a show, it is neither a dance nor a party, but it's the assemblage of a multitude of video images, songs, sounds and people, in a collective event in which each living for him or herself constitutes the other in parallel.

At the level of the performance we need to create some interplay via the rule of piracy; from the outset all navel-gazing must be abolished. Kaprow spoke of such a utopia: "Only when active artists willingly cease to be artists can they convert their abilities, like dollars into yen, into something the world can spend: play. Play as a currency. We can best learn to play by example, and un-artists can provide it."[3] "Converting one's own abilities" means being able to barter them, resell them, to acquire others and to really change. Piracy isn't make-believe, it definitively changes the identity of the player. The "interplay" in the performance stops being a system of theatrical interpretation and becomes precisely its opposite: an immersion in reality. This complicity between the fictional and the real is related to through a designed participation of the public. Rather it occurs through the creation of a context that allows what could be called a "conversion of abilities". This conversion is not synonymous with identification. The participants in the event do not simply share their abilities by confronting the other's identity with their own: they reciprocally steal each other's skills according to a logic of piracy. If Rancière taught us the lesson that contemporary society is composed from a separation of roles, activities and "parts"—a separation which structures the community in a hierarchical order—such a sharing is transformed into piracy when a disturbance occurs in the physical matter of the community itself. If sharing supposes division and identification, piracy supposes that some differentiation is at work even within the equalization of powers and knowledge. It's not so much a question of installing a "translation" of experiences, as Rancière wishes, but rather of a practice of abduction where nothing is translated or transformed but all is conserved in a process of accumulation.[8] The "stories of frontiers to be crossed and the distribution of roles to be blurred" does not stop at the "reorganization of [the spectators and performers] on the basis of equality", like the masters and the ignorant, the philosophers and the workers—but also attempts to safeguard the differences, to conserve the irreducible tensions.[9] In this manner, what is strictly untranslatable can quite easily pass from one body to another via this action of abduction, without such a passage making it intelligible. I can thus be a master of what I am ignorant of, just as I can steal from the master something he knows without, for all that, transforming my ignorance into knowledge.

Far from any fantasy of a renewed or emancipated society, the context of this kind of spectacle is both open and self-deprecatory. From the moment in which social identities are dissolved in a "coming community", in Agamben's words, the theatre is vaccinated against any enterprise of emancipation. Less pretentious but more effective, *©oPirates* exemplifies the possibilities and expectations of a theatricality which is autonomous yet completely anchored within the social fabric. This theatricality is thus "generic" or "anything whatsoever", since it is formed on the piracy of singularities: "Anything whatsoever is the form of pure singularity."[10] Of course, a society made up of indeterminate singularities is utopian. It is the utopia of a society in which egos and brutal forces are forever quiet, of an assembly of dolls. A huge emotion invades me. That completely kitsch image, there all of a sudden in the middle of this party surprises me. The video images come to a stop. The curtain is drawn back further, the music drops almost to silence.

A white space opens up behind the stage. Spectators sit—tired by this race, by all these dances and emotions—gathered together in a sacred place, sharing a moment of respite and rest. I sit down too, like a good little girl who gets off the merry-go-round with her head still spinning. At that moment singular figures start to walk in front of me: an ethereal dancer rises up in a subtle spiral; a singer with a powerful voice emits lyrical sounds in a language I don't recognize; a well-muscled man slides beneath the curtain; a woman walks, balancing on her head an enormous white ball that is so light, so light ... In the silence a group of men and women on roller skates arrive, pursuing each other in an infinite circle. And then I see people from the audience get up and join the group on the stage, as if pulled by a centripetal force. Everybody joins together in a final celebration, a common sharing. The curtain is drawn in close to us, surrounding us, pushing everyone towards the bar at the entrance. The party continues to the end of the night.

I leave, blown away. The night air is sweet, I'm no longer so cold.

of a sudden, instead of having to lead the spectators, I'm transported by them. Gestures are transmitted from one body to another; I see a complete stranger next to me clumsily pull off a sequence of movements that I master perfectly after having learnt it during rehearsals.

The dance spreads rapidly, like a virus; it sinks into the veins of the human bodies and flows like a river across a landscape. It rises, it falls, it decelerates, even stops for a moment, then takes another route and splits, drops back down again, it beats hard, then stagnates, exhausts itself and then surges back to the surface with extraordinary force. Completely unplanned performances emerge in the midst of this movement and we're all taken up in a collective whirlwind without beginning or end. A shared energy, an unusual amusement that is both natural and controlled, genuine emotion: this is a pleasure worthy of its name.

"happenings" where "doing a performance is accomplishing something, and not playing a role like in the theatre; moving some furniture for example, doing it for the sake of doing it, or doing it because you are moving house."[4] Reality and fiction are mixed together in this performance through the ludic spirit of piracy.

The plastic material confronting me also makes me think of Anna Halprin's "task-like dances", Yvonne Rainer's *Continuous Project/ Altered Daily* (1970) and Xavier Le Roy's *Projet* (2003)—all works of gestural appropriation, in which the dancer borrows her movements from everyday routines, natural behaviour and sport. The identity of the work—if it can still be called a work—is therefore impossible to discern inasmuch as each gesture lacks a specific identity and its own intentionality. It is impossible to know whether the performer is "pretending" to have fun, or whether he is actually having fun. In *©oPirates* it is impossible to discern the performers, because they are so mixed up with the spectators. The confusion between the supposed artifice of theatricality and the supposed reality of ordinary life produces a new kind of spectacle. At the same time as being the result of "fictional circumstances", the performance does produce a real party, and this by means of real gestures. Piracy brings about a genuine sharing, without camouflaging the tensions and difficulties that emerge amidst the collective.

individuals respectful of their differences, according to a logic of equity in which struggle and domination will have already been surpassed. It is a society made up of "solitudes" in Sartre's sense: projects and individual behaviours being formed in the heart of society.

Like any theatre worthy of its name, *©oPirates* illustrates the very structure of contemporary community and attempts to make spectators aware of its constitutive mechanisms. But this consciousness does not add anything to what already happens in normality. So the show becomes the mirror of the social fabric, a kind of living representation of contemporary industry's means of production; a reproduction of the conversion of abilities which structure human exchanges. Paolo Virno in his work emphasizes that "in a situation in which the means of production are not reducible to machines but consist of linguistic-cognitive competencies inseparable from living labour, it is legitimate to assume that a conspicuous part of the so-called 'means of production' consists of techniques and communicative procedures."[11] Piracy has thus already taken place amidst a post-Fordist society, where there is no longer any material capital, strictly speaking, a society organized around skills and knowhow, in which the role of the body becomes primordial, in which capital is henceforth identified with a singular ability, with a performance. Art thus comes to reflect reality and *©oPirates* places itself as much on a sociological as an artistic terrain.

The community thus becomes a "multitude" in which different manners of being together fuse in a diffuse practice of piracy. The citizen-worker and member of this community possesses the abilities proper to pirates, performers and athletes: "To be accustomed to mobility, to be able to keep up with the most sudden conversions, to be able to adapt to various enterprises, to be flexible in switching from one set of rules to another, to have an aptitude for a kind of linguistic interaction as banalized as it is unilateral, to be familiar with managing among a limited amount of possible alternatives."[12] Piracy is constructed on the basis of the circulation of identities whilst allowing the frictions, ruptures and migratory displacements that are specific to a multiple community. Piracy is a critique of the notion of private property and is placed not on the side of emancipation, but on the side of ordinary action, of what is already being fabricated in the side corridors, often hidden, of society.

1 The original French title is *Le Piratage du sensible* which is a play on words referring to the title of Jacques Rancière's famous book *Le Partage du sensible* (Paris: La Fabrique, 2000).
2 In English in the original.
3 Allan Kaprow, *The Blurring of Art and Life*, ed. Jeff Kelley (Berkeley: University of California Press, 1993).
4 Ibid.
5 Giorgio Agamben, *The Coming Community*, translated by Michael Hardt, (Minneapolis, MN: University of Minnesota Press, 1993), CH. I, CH. V.
6 Jean-Paul Sartre, *Critique de la raison dialectique*. Tome I. *Théories des ensembles pratiques* (Paris: Gallimard, Collection Bibliothèque de Philosophie, 1960), page 363. See *Critique of Dialectical Reason*, VOL. I, translated by Alan Sheridan-Smith (London: Verso, 2004). Part D Collectives (first three pages).
7 Ibid.
8 Jacques Rancière, *The Emancipated Spectator*, translated by Gregory Elliott (London: Verso, 2009).
9 Ibid.
10 Agamben, *The Coming Community*, CH. XVI.
11 Paolo Virno, *A Grammar of the Multitude: For an Analysis of Contemporary Forms of Life*, translated by Isabella Bertoletti, James Cascaito, and Andrea Casson (New York: Semiotext(e), 2004), page 61.
12 Ibid., pages 84–85.

BARBARA FORMIS

Ph.D. is Assistant Professor of Philosophy in the Department of Plastic Arts and Sciences of Art in the University Paris I, Panthéon-Sorbonne. In 2010 she published *Esthétique de la vie ordinaire* (Aesthetics of Ordinary Life) in the collection Lignes d'art for the Presses Universitaires de France. She also edited two anthologies: *Gestes à l'œuvre* (Gestures at Work) published by L'Incidence éditions at the end of 2008 and *Penser en corps* (Thinking Through the Body) published at the end of 2009 by L'Harmattan. She is the co-founder (with Mélanie Perrier) of the Laboratoire du Geste (Gesture Laboratory), a platform which promotes research, publication, and creation in the field of the performing arts. She was responsible for external seminars at the Collège International de Philosophie and a researcher in the Theory Department of the Jan van Eyck Academie in Maastricht. She has published many articles in journals such as *Art Press*, *La Revue d'esthétique*, *Multitudes*, *Alter* and *La Part de l'Œil*. She was also a dancer and in 2010, together with Chantal Pontbriand, co-dramaturge of Richard Siegal's piece *©oPirates*.

DRAGGING A MAN OUT OF HIS TORPOR
— Didier Faustino

She is really small, tiny. Like a pebble in the midst of all these trees. Quick glance roundabout, nothing seductive. Apart from her size, really small ... Steps, a door, a corridor leading to some empty rooms. A smell: damp, mouldiness; not a lot. Yes, the absinthe reflection of the bark through dirty windows.

My task is to remove the wooden boards forming the drawing room floor. Wood from Brazil, he told me. He'll be back to fetch me in the evening, then he'll salvage everything before the place is demolished. Silence and cold, already.

I start freeing the boards and I feel the sweat breaking out. All this dust, this trace of life and abandonment fills me with every gesture. My nose and throat, especially, are full of the dirt that I'm atoning for, for better or worse. I look with disgust at the black pebbles but then I get back to the laborious work.

Without even realizing it, I reach the last board. It's like the last button on a dress hiding a body that's been aged by time: the nakedness which is revealed is radiant and desolate all at once. After taking everything to the front door, I return to that forlorn body. My muscles are tight and I imagine the rub of blood in my veins. My eye undresses the room this time and I tell myself that I've finally made my bed there. I sit against the wall, near the window. The red and yellow on the bleached paper fascinate me. I hadn't noticed them first time around. By dint of looking at them and trying to guess what they smell like, I feel my body becoming drowsy. Too tired. I must stretch out and lie down; it doesn't matter about the dust. Sleep, well-being.

The yellow flowers bend in the wind and I hear a voice far off. I am uneasy, I look around me. The voice is clearer now. I recognize it: it's him, but I can't see him. In fact I can't see anything any more. Dark. Night. It's night. He's near me, waiting for me to get up. With difficulty I put my feet on the ground.

We'll be back tomorrow to fetch the wood.

There are more than ten rooms, all as arrogant as each other. I don't have any preference: this one, that one, it doesn't matter. Light everywhere, a digest of bourgeois culture; the furniture is draped with transparent plastic film, as if to tell me that looking is all that's permitted.

Like a peeping tom, I walk from room to room, and install myself within the Other. But this seduction must not make me forget why I'm here ... Pull down the wall separating the blue bedroom from the bathroom, to make just one room ...

A desire to cause damage fills me: wounding such a perfect thing. Premeditated pleasure.

The blows rain down carefully, but the temptation to change things is there. Violence, repeated hammering, rage. The first cracks in this wall which resists are followed by total dismantling, in the end without too much effort. My desire to fight is triggered. Frustration.

Hope: I must empty the bathroom of everything. The spotless enamel makes the initial arrogance of the house ring out and it irks me. The violence of the sledge hammer hardly scratches the parts, colliding with an unsuspected force. Dull noise, nothing. The premises are defending themselves. Great energy and fury. The first breach, at last, announces danger: bits and pieces fly in every direction like sparks. It doesn't matter, I'll finish it off. The cast iron breaks with that typical smell of metal against metal which goes to my head. This time it's the right one. My blow falls, badly. I feel the back of my hand slip along the clean break. Blade. The first instants of enraged pleasure at having won mix with a sudden sensation of softness and pain ... A warm red liquid runs along my fingers. Marking time.

Lots of people must have lived here. It seems huge, but what impressed me most, when I arrived, was the two buildings at the sides. Especially the right-hand one with its stables on the ground floor.

We came to bring the equipment for the team in charge of restoring the central part. Unloading the truck, lots of effort, quick breathing. Noon. Lunch time. Everyone gathers around the hot dishes but I don't have any appetite. No hunger ...

An odd thing. I slip away to explore this building which is forever catching my attention. The stables ... vast, the staircase giving onto the courtyard, the upper floor ... Row of rooms where my footsteps ring out. Sweet smell of wear and tear, dust; the whole thing envelops me. A winding flight of steps leads me up under the roof, towards my quest. What quest? While the others are still eating, the wood cracks under my feet. This excess of sensation heightens the mystery and makes me want to be even nosier. Here, a small, discreet room. On each side of the endless corridor, bedrooms ... Landscapes pinned to the wall, crimson photographs, cobwebs and old mattresses haunt the place. I must visit them all and lend an ear. In this one, nothing. Ten feet by six with a small opening in the roof. The wall. Covered with pictures of naked bodies. The colours have faded, but the poses can be deciphered without any difficulty. Another bedroom. No. My curiosity has given way to excitement: I'm looking for something else. My lower abdomen is burning, I must go back into the room with the naked bodies. I take a close look at the pictures. Anxiety. Don't make any noise, no surprises. My buttocks rest on the dirty cold floor. Detail. The gesture becomes faster. Elsewhere ... Fleeting pleasure ... Private fluids mixed with the dust.

Alone, in some one else's bedroom. I walk through the door. The moment has gone.

NEEDS

For almost an hour I've been desperate ... Foul weather.

The room with the mod cons is situated at the far end of the land. The very idea of walking through all that mud chills me. But what I have inside me is bothering me more and more. I need some paper.

Here, nothing but rough walls, mineral. Just mineral. A house construction site without a corner to accommodate my needs. There, an old cement bag. I don't care. I won't be back tomorrow. Do it behind this pile of sand, away from prying eyes. It's just a building site, after all. What will become of it? A bedroom, a kitchen? Not knowing. Not able to ... foul weather.

Take the old bag anyway, arrange it properly and keep a bit to wipe myself. Rough, aggressive sensation, but relief.

Conscientiously I grab the whole thing to throw it through the hole in the wall–future window–as there isn't a hole in the floor. Wall, floor, inside, outside. What's the difference?

Yet I can't leave any other way, leaving this house to be built on filth. Sympathetic trace, indelible but invisible ...

I sow forever and ever and go away satisfied.

Branco is neither an artist nor an architect. He's working in the building trade. From house to house, he constructs and destroys things. He is there before and after our effects, brushing against what hasn't belonged to him, and won't belong to him, without understanding it. However, each instant that is his makes him master of the premises. Being invisible to fleeting unions, he gives fast, in his own way. Branco is neither an artist nor an architect.

Dragging A Man Out Of His Torpor, Revised text, Anticorps. Didier Fuiza Faustino/Bureau des Mésarchitectures, published by HYX— Collection Frac centre, 2004.

DIDIER FAUSTINO

Artist and architect, Didier Faustino works on the intimate relationship between body and space. His approach is multifaceted, from installation to experimentation, from the creation of subversive visual art to spaces challenging the senses.

Didier Faustino created the Bureau des Mésarchitectures in 2002 and received the Académie d'Architecture's Dejean prize for lifetime achievement in 2010.

He has been honored several times with the Chernikhov Prize (Moscow), has participated in numerous biennials (Venice, Taipei, Yokohama, Sao Paulo, Istanbul, Beijing, etc.), and created Evento, a new artistic and urban event in Bordeaux, in 2009.

His iconic works include: *Hermès H Box* (2006), a mobile video screening hall to be presented in museums worldwide (Tate Modern in London, the Pompidou Centre in Paris, the Beyeler Foundation in Basel, etc.), *Body in Transit* (2000), a minimal space criticizing the transport of illegal immigrants, presented at the Venice Biennale and featured in collections of the Pompidou Centre, *Double Happiness* (2009), a set of two swings in the air at the Shenzhen-Hong Kong Biennial, *Révolution(s)* (2004), a chrysalis ceiling for the Museum of Modern Art of the City of Paris presented to the Cordeliers Convent, and *Sky is the Limit*, (2006), a tea room lifted to twenty meters above the ground near the Korean DMZ. He is currently working on several projects around the world.

AGAINST A HYGIENAPOLIS
— Didier Faustino

There is a city where bodies no longer exist.

Needless to say, it is peopled with human beings who live and walk about, but bodies properly so called no longer have their place in it. This is the Hygienapolis.

In Hygienapolis, everything is polished and smooth, everything is product, and everything is similar. The unforeseen is banned, precisely because it is unforeseen. The norm reigns, perfection is the model. Everything must work like well-oiled clockwork: there must be airports for aircraft, railway stations for trains, roads for vehicles, places for work, places to have fun in, places to live in, for people on the move, people who produce, and people who consume. The loop has come full circle. Hygienapolis, as you will have gathered, is everywhere and nowhere all at once. It is the virus which lies in wait for us, because we have wanted to get ahead too much, without thinking, at the risk of forgetting why we want to put one foot in front of the other, relentlessly. It is this pseudo-quest for time and relevance which haunts the urbs in which we are evolving. Always faster, always more beautiful. It is this obsession with "what shall we do?" which lingers on the "do" without considering the "what".

To counter this Hygienapolis we need to propose antibodies. Antibodies for the body. Antibodies for the space.

These antibodies are projects which, like illegal substances, free the individual—and architecture—of inhibitions. As territories of all manner of possibility, they reinvent the link between each other for a twofold revelation: of space through the body and of the senses through architecture. At the risk of looking like a mirage and of being the falsehoods of custom, they are there to fight and arouse. For we do not envisage architecture without struggle and combat. And if we need to run away from the (architectural) posture, it is the better to understand our position and include ourselves in a reality, in an actuality that runs counter to virtuality.

To this end, we need to espouse doubt, the doubt that haunts and drives. That fault which, once discovered, merely becomes more lovely and more precious. This dysfunction to be grasped in order to produce "lecherous architectures"[1] and place oneself in the interstice. Not beside, not any old where, just between. Between two suburban houses, between two bodies, between a body and the inhabited space.

But the interstice is also the "place left vacant",[2] the space of freedom and, consequently, of possible transgression. Use and abuse. Use sense to abuse the senses. Use physicality to abuse common sense, that decoy of propriety. For by dint of indulgence, we reach violence. Violence of a so-called ethics which has more going for it than aesthetics. But through what intervention is aesthetics the smooth, the neutral? Be beautiful and shut up? No, it's not that. Go beyond the question of appearance, of skin. We're not plastic ... surgeons, still less do we go in for packaging. To all those WYSWYGs[3] we reply that there is much more to see and get. Everything depends on the viewpoint—and the focus. There is no auto-focus; we put ourselves in the depth of field. Field, narrative. To do that, it is true, we have to use a certain triviality of form. Evidence of a body turned in on itself, evidence of a piece of a standard jigsaw puzzle. No need to weigh yourself down with convoluted forms or produce by means of technological tangents what the mind itself cannot conceive of alone. We are not looking for this particular justification and remuneration. Without doing away with any of the eye's pleasure, we prefer to be on the outer edge of aesthetic truism, for this immediacy in the primary, formal reading is only there to better serve the subject. If we lay claim to no wisdom, or any dogmatism whatsoever, we do, on the contrary, assert a stance. Each project assumes a viewpoint, mine, and we should reveal ourselves a little bit more. The risk is there and we have to take it. The involvement resides in what we have as individuals, in harmony and not in harmony; not in the defence of a Cause, no matter how noble it might be. Getting beyond the instant, so as not to forget time passing, time which goes beyond us. Architecture is far from being frozen and cannot conceive of itself as such. If the freeze frame is at times necessary, or at least useful, it must not mask the motion which accompanies the architectured space in all its complexity. Architecture also dies, but above all it lives. It lives at the pace of those using it, for which it has been planned. It is no coincidence if the imagery of the instructions for use is sometimes present, if projects often break down into spare parts. They are only there to serve and could never be sufficient unto themselves. Their value, if any there be, only appears when they are used and in their capacity to reveal, to create an awareness of a situation, even if it means forcing the line.

These are our desires, these are our needs.
Desire for the unforeseen, desire for vices. Need for doubt and endangerment.
For soluble objects and fathomless bodies.
An architecture under the influence.

1 Hervé Guibert, *Vice* (Paris: éditions Jacques Bertoin, 1991), "Rules and Regulations" chapter, page 43. Translated by Simon Pleasance.

"The city and the State would now have to organize a certain number of vacant places, with the sole aim of accommodating lecherous and libertine little acts, particularly luxurious with regard to the waste of time they cause citizens.

Props and sets would be installed at the bends of certain streets, on plots of waste ground, in houses being demolished, in wrongly abandoned theatres, secretly maintained. False nights would follow false heat waves, temporal exoticisms and differing latitudes, creating in the city a whole ludic and excessively mobile itinerary. Other places, set up from scratch would vanish as soon as the vice has been consumed: they would be like traps set, but pleasure traps; some enthusiasts would illegally cobble things together in accordance with their personal fantasies, and hide until someone comes to honour their imagination. Vice would become a free public service. The State would hold competitions which would reward the creators of architecture and novel lecherous machines."

2 Ibid.

3 What You See is What You Get

DIDIER FAUSTINO

The biography of Didier Faustino can be found next to page 24.

METAL POSTCARD
— Tim Etchells

Metal is tough, metal will sheen
Metal won't rust when oiled and cleaned
Metal is tough, metal will sheen
Metal will rule in my master scheme

Metal Postcard/Mittageisen
Siouxsie And The Banshees, 1978.

INTRODUCTION

It's a long story even to get to the title. I was seventeen years old. We lived on the outskirts of Derby—a kind of shit town in the Midlands of England. When my brother was approaching his fifteenth birthday, my friends and I—all a year or so older than me—devised a plan to kidnap him.

We put a bag over Mark's head, I think, and bundled him into the back of a car belonging to a friend—we drove him blindfold like that for fifty miles and then let him out in the car park of a music venue. The gig was Siouxsie And The Banshees. That was Mark's fifteenth birthday present.

I won't assume that anyone knows the Siouxsie And The Banshees album from 1978—their first album, titled *The Scream*. It was something I played again and again at the time. One of those times/places when an album connects ... if not to the actual world you're living in, then at least to the psychic landscape you inhabit. It was pretty much all harsh sounds—shrill voice, screeching, tearing guitars, but at the same time very tight, martial almost, very clean, sharp, acidic. I guess an odd mix of emotion, desperation, desire for escape, on the one hand, and clinical clarity on the other.

Some way into the gig they played a song called "Metal Postcard/Mittageisen"—the title a nonsense term based on the German word *Mittagessen* for "lunch"—which can be translated as "noon iron". Dedicated to the DADA artist John Heartfield the song was written as a response to his image *Hurrah, the Butter is Finished!* (1935).

Born in 1891 in Berlin as Helmut Herzfeld, Heartfield changed his name in 1916, to criticize the nationalism and anti-British sentiment prevalent in Germany during World War I. In the 1920s and 1930s, working for the *Arbeiter Illustrierte Zeitung (AIZ)* workers' illustrated paper, his collages focused visual attacks on the rising National Socialist Party. After Hitler became Chancellor in 1933, Heartfield left Germany and continued from Prague. Working in collaboration with his brother Wieland Herzfelde and others, Heartfield staged photographs subsequently cutting them together, collaging or superimposing negatives to create a single "scene".

In *Hurrah, the Butter is Finished!* Heartfield starts from Hermann Göring's statement concerning food shortages in Germany: "Iron ore makes an empire strong—butter and lard just make it fat."

With the butter all gone, the family in the image enthusiastically sets about a meal of assorted metal fragments—bicycle chain, tools, an axe and other detritus. It's an image of the family—seated and eating the products of an industrial system—an image of eating as starvation, mechanistic, brutal—a picture of the family in Fascism, showing the impossibility of human survival in a militarized, industrialized, mechanized landscape.

In writing to this image Siouxsie takes us from Heartfield and Germany in the 1930s to the depressed wasteland and domestic scene of Britain in 1976, the family seated now in the living room, not eating at the table, but gathered to watch the TV, drinking (mercury), and waiting for another news bulletin. Siouxsie's "Metal Postcard"—"Thought I'd drop a line, the weather here is fine"—steps us into a hall of mirrors—as much future as it is the present of 1976, it's in any case a future via Orwell whose 1984 was as much 1948 as it was a future. In short, Siouxsie steps us into a hall of mirrors of social, political and media control, the starvation diet of metal she describes at once a liquid, acoustic, visual and informational one.

Reunion begins
With a glass of mercury
Whilst television flickers
For another news bulletin
Flints light up the eyes
Of the seated family

Metal is tough, metal will sheen
Metal won't rust when oiled and cleaned
Metal is tough, metal will sheen
Metal will rule in my master scheme

Fresh out of his blindfold,
I think my brother Mark was impressed.

PROCESS

Not so much works as investigations or processes set in motion; enquiries, conceptual machineries, social exchanges and their effects.

Not so much artists in some old sense, but rather networks and collaborations, the rippling out of effects from social and conceptual artistic machineries—artistic/social interventions initiated and then maintained.

Or, the same thing by another route. Not so much genius in the sense of a virtuosic or highly idiosyncratic assembly of signifiers but rather such genius as might be demonstrated in curating a flow, conceiving and convening a meeting, permissioning an exchange, corralling persons, presences, data. The skill of the analyst, curator, party planner or networker, catalyst, agent, switching station.

Frames created in order to facilitate meeting, discussion, encounter, exchange. Works whose content comes not through something inserted by the artist, but by/through the actions of participants. Relational Aesthetics. Audiences that are at the same time performers. Knowledge Exchange.

CONTEXTS

No so much *a* context for art but rather *contexts* for action and intervention. The art of moving items from one frame to another. Social frames, institutional frames, political frames. Affecting the circumstances and situation of visibility. Perhaps that's what art always was/is?

ARCHIVE

Not so much creations, visions, flights of fancy as a landscape of observations, remixes or data rescued from the flow. Thinking of data, or more explicitly of archive, a shift perhaps, as some have observed, from the period of making to the period of assessing what has already been made. The study of the data pile. With the so-called-real pressed, pulled or in any case logged into digital space, work now proceeds on the endlessly accumulating archive, artefacts, documents and real-time traces. As if, one might say, enough has been made, enough has happened, what's needed is to make some assessment of the backlog. To kick over the traces.

ARCHIVE II (NO DISAPPEARANCE)

After all, documents multiply. For every event an ever larger smear of ghosts to follow it and as the cultural data pile/archive gets larger, the task of making-sense—navigation/navigation tools—becomes more and more vital.

In the specific case of performance, we shift from the few enigmatic black and white stills of something like Chris Burden's *Shoot* piece in 1976 to a place where each performance rests after the fact in a shallow grave comprising innumerable fragments and traces dispersed as video, downloadable image files, YouTube clips, and a thousand circulating documents, blog accounts and texts. No more the truly ephemeral, if such it ever was, no more the fading, disappearing edge or phantasm of performance. Instead performance as a permanent half-life of fragments and traces. Not disappearance but a continuous afterlife in the largely digital museum of slivers, traces, parts. No more disappearance in fact.

REGARDING FICTION

A strange situation:

On the one hand, truth—the truth of truth—is everywhere doubted. All-purpose scepticism, conspiracies abound/things are not what they seem, events seen through the surrounding political spin, news, and media spectacle are all but universally suspected. No one owns up to believing anything anymore.

At the same time, fiction has little status either—since "fiction in general", "pretending" and "theatre" are all objects of derision/suspicion, perhaps in good part because of any role they might have played in unsettling the king "truth". Fiction—as corrupt, as source of suspicion—is in any case a hangover from modernism; any thing theatrical is seen as a debasing of purist forms and aspirations.

Between these two poles though—truth and fiction—with uncanny persistence it is the real, or its phantasm, that still holds a strong grip on the collective imagination.

Suspicious of the fiction in theatre, we see instead all kinds of documentary dramas. From the plays based on trial or public inquiry transcripts to the person-dramas constructed around the lives or presences of "found" individuals explored in works by Stefan Kaegi, Lola Arias, Ant Hampton, Quarantine etc. From Jerôme Bel's de-skilled choreographies to his documentary portraits like *Veronique Doisneau* through to Forced Entertainment projects like *The Travels*, which set a real-world process in motion, then report on the results—endless collections of texts, stories, songs, photographs donated by others or garnered from interview. The authority at base comes from the real—from things which have reportedly happened.

STRATEGIES OF AUTHORSHIP

Suspicious of individual authorship, we see collaborative works, not the collective creative collaboration that emerged as a political strategy in theatre in the 1960s, so much as works summoned from a participating network and innumerable processual/gathering projects, which solicit materials from others. From the Internet economy—crowd sourcing. Again—a privileging of the curatorial or collecting impulse—the gathering and subsequent arrangement of data.

PARTICIPATION

Suspicious of the bugbear one-way communication (the theatre frame), a preponderance instead of interactive projects, open not just to the interpretational intervention of the spectator, but to her contribution/choices/moves/navigations/actions/decisions in a game. Punch Drunk, Coney, Blast Theory in England, for example. The authority comes from the real again—not so much in the "reality" of whatever worlds are presented/represented/used as backdrops for these structures—but from the much valorized authentic participation of actual persons whose circulation, dynamic intervention, decisions, behaviours, energies in a certain sense are the work.

CRITIQUE OF THE MARKET

Much has been made of performance's historical resistance, question or explicit critique to the market—its insistence on its own passing, its own particular moment, its transience, its lack of saleable object. It's a critique that applies in a very particular context—visual arts—but which struggles to find traction in the zones of theatre-performance or dance. Differences arise from the construction of markets in these contexts but since art proper concerns itself with selling objects, the initial challenge of a more ephemeral practice, such as performance, is clear.

Theatre and dance, however, have long been economies based on selling the ephemeral—events, rather than objects. A challenge to the market structure in these forms comes inevitably, therefore, through different routes. At one level, since the 1960s, experimental theatre and contemporary dance have challenged the transferable market of "the play" by laying emphasis on the connection between authors (makers, devisors, creators) and performers—people performing their own work, work that's been based in and built on the unique set of physicalities, presences, identities of the artists and not suitable for transmission into a more generalized economy. In these cases, after all, there's no play-text that can be re-made by other theatres or directors, there's no scored and transmittable dance which can be versioned by others. A version of Raimund Hoghe's work with Faustin Linyekula performed by someone else makes no sense. Theatrical has removed authority—author is an absent god—performance, meanwhile, asserts the authority and singularity of the present artist whose body, actions and intentions are cohered. A further challenge to the traditional theatre market of reproducible plays comes once again from the creation of the kind of exchanges, "unstable" or open ended events that are produced through one-off encounters of performers, decisions and interactions of audiences and so on.

Meanwhile, returning to the visual arts and the initial challenge of performance to the object-based economy, we have to note that, from the outset, performance has pretty much always spawned the document, trace or residue, and that the document, trace or residue can always be editioned and sold.

Indeed, since the last decades of the twentieth century and early part of the twenty-first, art history, art practice and the market have all taken steps to rake over the traces, documents and residual objects of performance from the previous heyday of the 1960s and 1970s, a process which has gone hand in hand with the ongoing monetization of the supposed problem-child performance.

Speaking of the "value of performance" in the present cultural moment we might well dwell on Warhol's focus on media, celebrity and self-presentation, his equation of artist and name, his performance of artist as brand-name. Accumulating value in this sense—for the arts as for all markets—is about brand profile and recognition, and the impact or place of an artist and her work is as much about the fantasy of associations it triggers as it is about actual works. Performance, especially in the visual arts context, might at worst be understood as a loss-leader in establishing or developing a brand via a performative presence in social and actional space. Performance—although it might (sometimes) create no objects—nonetheless creates unique cultural capital through the event, creating artist identity, brand, profile and market-ready position. The objects can come later. The event pushes the name and the name can always be monetized later, adding value to the name itself and to the cultural institutions or collections with which it is connected.

A hairdresser in New York describing to an acquaintance of mine, with great glee, his planned trip to MOMA where, in his words, "this lady sits at a table every day and you can go to sit across from her to have a staring contest." He's describing Marina Abramović' *The Artist is Present* from last year—though neither name is one that he has heard—not the artist and not the title of the piece. He just knows about the staring contest.

Even those artists—Tino Sehgal—whose hankerings after ephemerality border on the obsessive/comical—are in some senses perhaps establishing a fetish of the real/ephemeral—the non-recorded, non-objectified status of the work an effective and playful tool in the development of its notoriety and the raising of its eventual price, come the day of the concept-sale. Sehgal tests the system to its limit, circulating his work in a way that seems designed to make visible the process of exchanging money for pure idea.

At the same time, artists from the former era with a reputation built on actions can also cash in their chips in the contemporary frame in the mode of later auto-reflection and re-visiting. The most peripheral, invisible actions and practices can be recuperated and, put simply—what we all know anyway—there is nothing which can't eventually be monetized if the will or interest to do so is there. The market will find a way.

Certainly, in the last twenty years, with the witting collaboration of living artists and the unwitting collaboration of the dead, performance has become a space of relics, replicas and frequent re-visitings—the curatorial and art historical impulse to readdress/re-frame and re-tell the history working in tandem with the market's resourceful monetizing of what could be salvaged from the wreckage, combined in a way that should leave no room for doubt concerning capitalism's ability to meet and absorb the supposed critique offered by performance proper, in the visual arts context.

THE BROADER CONTEXT

The emergence of new forms, processes of incorporation/appropriation of performance, arrives alongside the emergence of what's called variously social, cognitive or information capitalism (and a lot of other things besides). Where once capitalism was largely about the manufacture, distribution and sale of things—objects—or perhaps services, it's shifted ground more recently to concern itself increasingly with more nebulous (though no less lucrative) acts of creation, distribution and sale.

Capitalism in its new mode is socially networked, processual and ever more bound up with the intangible. It is also deeply performative in that it generates its "products" through the corralled energy of people's participation, time-investment and collective fantasy. Selling ideas or processes via the right or licence to take part in or activate them rather than selling things as such (for example software or digital music), selling participation, selling data gathered through keeping track of participation, selling access, and in the end, in short form, selling the idea, feeling and experiences of belonging along with the fantasy of self-determination.

Seen from here—in the rotten heart of the experience economy—performance cannot be so readily framed as it once was, as a threat to the intellectual underpinnings or operational principles of the market. Indeed, neither performance's connection to the intangible, its ephemerality, its base in process or its relational construction mark it as different from what surrounds it in the commercial sector where post-Fordist capitalism already asks us to purchase what we will, in one sense, make ourselves, celebrates and exploits our desire for ephemeral experiences, encouraging us to tailor-make, participate in or customize them, assuming and demanding that we define ourselves as much through these acts or processes as through what we own.

What perhaps neither John Heartfield or Siouxsie Sioux knew was quite how deep inside us all that metal would get. Or how molten, fragmented, solvent, dispersible and pervasive it would prove to be.

Heartfield imagined a brutalizing toxic encounter between the human body and the products of mass production, and Siouxsie, thirty-seven years later, rewrote this narrative as an encounter between the human mind and the voices or forces of top-down media communications—the TV news, the loudspeakers in the song, which spill voices blaring from the street-corners.

The metal though is not so much liquid as it is pixels now. Production mostly concerned with the circulation of ideas and energies. Everything flows, moves around. We're eating it all the time.

Captalism's fantasy is of resources deployed endlessly in ever new combinations that will never cease to excite, delight but never quite satisfy. It's a fantasy of endless acquisition, built on the idea that every experience and relation is something ownable, purchasable, graspable, commodifiable. It's also a fantasy of world without end—built on the death-denying idea that none of this has to stop, that none of it will run out. But we know that's not true.

What's interesting to me is that the model of networked capitalism and new models of performance based practices—dispersed, gathering, relational—are very much in step, bound together. Certainly, networked capitalism has paid good attention to the kinds of understanding about identity and meaning creation that emerged from counter cultures and avant-garde art practice in the late twentieth century.

Meanwhile, both social capitalism and contemporary performance practice are themselves intertwined with, and (to an extent) driven by, changes in the means of production and technological possibility—especially regarding digital media and the network—which in a literal sense have made possible new modes of collective remote or mediatized working, creating and experiencing. Most importantly though, as always these material technological changes have given rise to new understandings and intellectual frameworks—metaphors/ways of thinking—which have then shown directions for change and action in the material social sphere.

*

One of the most interesting things for me in the last decades has been the shift in the site of performance. This we've seen for a long time on the physical plane, such that many of the spaces dedicated to industrial mass-production—coal mines, like the one at PACT Zollverein in Essen, where this text was first presented, factories and so on—have been repurposed as arts, museum or other kinds of cultural space, if not to become lofts, flats and apartments. At the same time, performance has wandered offstage and into diverse locations, not least disappearing into the virtual realm, the head or the space of imagination.

I thought I'd drop a line.
The weather here is fine.

My 2001 SMS performance *Surrender Control* was an interactive work comprising an escalating sequence of text message instructions delivered direct to the mobile phones of individual users. Participants subscribed to the project by sending a message to a particular number and, from that point on, received a certain number of text message instructions over a specified time period (for example, seventy-five instructions over five days). Responding to the intimate context of the mobile phone and of SMS as a form of communication, *Surrender Control*, and the follow up project *39 or So to Do* created for Tanzquartier Wien in 2009, invited the user into an evolving game of textual suggestions, provocations and dares.

The instructions received by participants in these projects vary enormously: some are orders to think about particular topics; some are invitations to look at the world in a particular way; others order action, demanding that participants behave in particular ways or carry out particular tasks. Receiving these instructions directly to their phones in real time, as they go about their lives and work in different locations, participants in these SMS works, experience the intervention of the project in a "place" most commonly occupied by friends, family or lovers.

Rather than developing through narrative, the structure of the piece moved in terms of increasing demands and dares, i.e. it had a "pull to excess" or a "pull to the edges of the game that's established", which has often been a principal tactic in performance works that I've been involved in as director and writer. In both *Surrender Control* and *39 or So to Do* the texts become more and more insistent, stranger or more intrusive—they also became more frequent at times or else arrived at increasingly anti-social times of the day. Working to very different principles than *flashmob*, the project avoided spectacle or any kind of carnivalesque gathering or performative excess of participants. I aimed for a pluralistic or dispersed development—eschewing any sense of the work cohering around a single narrative idea. This is an observation I find myself making often about my work, in different media, insisting that I don't want it to collapse into narrative, preferring it to remains in that state of suspension where narratives are possible but not confirmed. Working with SMS is interesting in that (as with media like literature or music) one has little control—one's not in control concerning the context of reception, however much one wants to sculpt and the meaning of what one writes/sends is always changed by the context at the other end, reinvented/reassembled uniquely by each recipient.

Virtual events—including those described, invited or summoned by text message—have developed as a through line in my practice, which often seeks to explore the liberating and excessive possibilities that language offers as a means of production. From the theatre performance *Dirty Work* (1998) made with Forced Entertainment to videos like *Starfucker* (2001) to *100 People* (2007), I've tested the vividness of events produced in language and the collaborative (co-authorial) processes that draw readers/viewers into dynamic and imaginative relationships to the work as it unfolds.

Most recently, I've explored both the form of the pamphlet and the Internet as sites for particular kinds of virtual events summoned in language. In a series of works starting in 2009 with *Events at the Downturn* my "Events Booklets" and the Internet project *Vacuum Days* advertised series of events, combining political and theatrical spectacle, with impossible, absurd and satirical performances, lectures, contests and film screenings.

Running for the whole of 2011, starting on January 1 the most recent of these projects was the online extravaganza *Vacuum Days*, in which a new announcement was created each day responding to political and other current events. Mimicking the contemporary appetite for reality as cruel spectacle, *Vacuum Days* parroted phrases from tabloid headlines, Internet spam and talent contest announcements to both mirror and distort the contemporary landscapes of media and reality.

I thought I'd drop a line.
The weather here is fine.

I was trying to follow events on the Internet while I was writing much of this text. Started out in Tunis and Egypt ... then moved to Libya. This from early on in the Egyptian protests, when AP interviewed some protesters.

Radwa Qabbani, 26, said:

"I am not protesting against the police. They are citizens like me. I am protesting against corruption, unemployment and high prices. We are just asking for the smallest dreams."

I think this is a wonderful phrase.

WE ARE JUST ASKING
FOR THE SMALLEST DREAMS

Also from AP, a few days later:

"Protesters emerged stumbling from white clouds of tear gas, coughing and covering their faces with scarves. Some had blood streaming down their faces. One man fainted. Police dragged some away and beat a journalist, smashing her glasses and seizing her camera."

So far so completely generic. And then this:

"At one point, the protesters seemed to gain the upper hand, forcing a line of riot police to flee under a barrage of rocks. One demonstrator climbed into a fire engine and drove it away."

So now, with the fire engine parked up outside, it's time to make some demands.

Even knowing what we know above about the power of capital to contain and appropriate we continue to Demand that the event, as event, be truly un-incorporable/ Seek out, reach for, the impossible to incorporate. The event so riven with contradiction that it cannot be resolved. Resistance to closure. Negation of closure.

We are just asking for the smallest dreams.

The thing which resists your gaze, your inquiry, judgement, scrutiny and analysis. The gift leads me in a circle around itself, a blankness all of its own. Blankness.

Or as I wrote before:

Down with poisonous slickness, defensive seamlessness and rhetorical authority. We'd rather have the provisional, the vulnerable and the playful. We'd rather have the event that unfolds and unravels. We want intimacy, transformation, negotiation, subversion, provocation, teasing, exchange, exhaustion, confrontation, slipping, sliding, ephemerality and eye contact. Less than this is very likely bullshit.

You may sell the residues but the event—as memory, as actuality—remains deeply troubling.

We are just asking for the smallest dreams.

Perhaps not even the event so much, as the opening of space. A space in which meeting might take place.

*

My best guess is that there was a hint of what might be needed in that 1978 evening in Derby when we temporarily abducted my brother.

It was an action in the real space of a life—a small intervention, I'm not making big claims—something between the dynamics of teenage friendship and kinship—a prank in any case, a meaningless adventure, something to pass the time. But it carved out a space that did not quite belong to any logic, made the word sing in an unexpected way. Something there for me, about the space of performance.

From the concert itself not much stays with me though I think I remember the taste of it, the flavour and that S was amazing—the sound of her voice clipped, cutting, sharp, empty as it is on the recordings of her from that time.

There is one concrete moment in the concert that I remember for sure though. S was singing another song from the album *The Scream*. She was near the front of the stage, near the end of the song. The line I remember is a kind of desolate wondering if she might "kill myself or you"—you need her voice really, to make much sense of it. But what I remember is that she split the line very much—singing the "kill myself" out to the crowd, and that with the "or" she withdrew, collapsing her gaze onto herself, then crouching, tenderly at the front to sing the last part of the line "or you" direct to the kids pressed hard against the stage at the front. Playing the last line down to the audience. Very close, very intimate. Her turn closing this gap between the rhetoric of performance and the now of the moment.

There was a strange doubleness to this moment, of course. A kind of standard theatrics of the move from the epic address to the whole auditorium "kill myself" to some impossible kind of private address with the "or you". I'd maybe not seen that move from the crowd to the front row done so explicitly or so well until that moment, though I think I've seen it a million times since then but at that time I immediately understood something from it about the dynamic between performance as an experience that is at once collective and individual. But what only struck me as I've been thinking about that night for this text is that the "or [kill] you" creates a problem in the turn from one space to the other. Because there, in the direct appeal for intimacy—squatted at the front of the stage, ducking under its rhetoric, making contact, reaching out, open, human scale—is also a threat, a warning, an insistence suggesting the impossibility of meaningful or amicable contact or trust—as if the dream of direct contact already contains its own negation and destruction. Text and performance enter a kind of intensely contradictory relation, an unresolvable fight and at the same time a balancing act. The moment can't be contained, simply can't be put away.

In Siouxsie's turn—kill myself or you—in that gentle threat, there's an acknowledgement that freedom or liberation, creation and artistic fecundity are entwined in some way with the possibility of violence or violation. That the possibility of intimacy is both amazing and terrible, that escape contains a threat. Her turn—in performance—is *a kind of reckoning with that element.*

I wrote to my brother about the Banshees gig in 1978.

He said that he could only remember the feeling of afterwards
That in the days afterwards reality bent out of shape,
That the days were full of possibility.

That what he wanted were the smallest dreams.

He wrote that he wanted everything in fact but please let it not be that Utopia with doves and waterfalls and soft white clothes and doors that open as soon as they are approached
and please let it not be that utopia with all in harmony and accord
and please not that utopia of agrarian fantasy, with all of us in touch with or at peace with the land, working the land together or weaving together in some endlessly temperate and agreeable climate, caught in simple pleasures, eating simple wholesome food
and please—he wrote, please, just as strongly, please—let it not be that techno utopia where no one works at all since the machines—ever more clever, resourceful and skilled—are doing everything, hidden in basements, miniaturized or concealed behind the walls
and please not that morbid utopia that so many churches speak of or hope for or promise, but only come the day, meaning after death
and not that utopia of absolute freedom or that of total equality
or that of the flattening of creeds, races, genders and all that into one single humanity or brotherhood
he wrote and not that utopia of original ignorance, Adam and Eve, the nakedness that is not nakedness no thank you
and not that utopia of free love
or boundless and open desire
or that hallucinatory psychedelic utopia of the human dissolved into the universe
and not that utopia of the virtual, with its useless pretended transcendence of flesh and biology
and again please, he wrote, not that utopia of endless oneness and endless accord
not likely peace, or everlasting peace
not likely peace at all
and not the satisfaction of all desires
and not the exhaustion of all need
and he wrote, please not an end to difference

no to the utopia determined by sense
no to the utopia determined by utility
no to the utopias of knowledge, understanding, and progress
please not the uniformity of consent
or that of placidity
no to the erasure of anger
he wrote please not the utopic reduction of human space to that of a prison in which all
needs have been anticipated, prescribed, provided for
please not the reduction of everything to the realm of the solvable
please not some landscape of banality cotton-wooled and perpetuated ad nauseam
not late-capitalist laissez-faire bliss
not communistic brotherhood
not either theocratic order
or rationalist decency
not some medicalized or genetically modified utopia in which all personalities and physicalities have been balanced,
remixed and extended forever in a calculation of chemicals
and genes
please, he wrote, not the utopia of the old and wise
and please not that utopia of the young and the carefree
please he wrote
not men and women in accord with each other in all the possible combinations,
or mankind so called at accord once again with "the animals" so called
no, not equality, he wrote, not equality
nor comfort
nor acceptance
not even tolerance
we'll have none of it
a utopia of dispute might be better
a utopia of permanent contestation
anger and the unruly

but he wrote, not even those will satisfy

let's have instead the utopia which resists all names,
refuses all belonging
refuses all place, definition or affiliation
i.e.
not for us that which can be dreamed or imagined, described or spoken of
and not for us anything that can be caught in the noose of 26 letters (called an alphabet)
and hanged
not for us what is offered
not for us what is given
not for us what is promised
not for us what is even possible
not that
not anything of it
but everything, everything which is other than that

friends, acquaintances, enemies
he wrote, he looked forward to an eventual meeting,
and to the full acceptance of these
his most reasonable demands

Tim Etchells. January 2011 / Revised version: February 2012. Commissioned text for the international conference "Beyond Curating" at PACT Zollverein, Essen, January 28–30, 2011, curated by Sigrid Gareis, Stefan Hilterhaus, Christine Peters

TIM ETCHELLS

An artist and writer based in the UK whose work shifts between performance, visual art, and fiction. He has worked in a wide variety of contexts, notably as the leader of the world-renowned performance group Forced Entertainment.

He is currently Professor of Performance Writing at Sheffield University.

TOWARDS ANOTHER WORLD
Performativity and Ephemerality in the Works
— Chantal Pontbriand

In 2008, just as the subprimes crisis exploded, I was asked to do an exhibition for the Lhoist Collection. As I was looking through the collection's catalogues, I came upon a work by Sigmar Polke.[1] It particularly caught my attention. The photograph showed a man dressed in black, hands clasping the large tree trunk behind him. He seemed to be nudging himself into the trunk, hollowed out by old age and natural deterioration. It struck me that this image echoed the times, the fear and anxiety that had arisen in months before. The tree trunk seemed to serve the purpose of a refuge, although the man's gaze was projecting itself outwards, to an unspecified and unknown horizon.

This unspecified and unknown horizon was to become more and more symptomatic of life on earth as the years have passed since I encountered this image. The title Polke had given to this particular image and the series that it is part of is "Higher Powers Command" (it became the title of the exhibition). The world is at a loss as society is struck by major political and economic changes. As revolutions ferment in the Arab world, economic downfalls affect the financial health of corporations and countries in the West, while the Eastern European countries are still recovering from the collapse of the Iron Curtain; growth and modernization transform Asia, especially China and India, the new superpowers; and our individual existences are troubled by a loss of predictable values, constant change, a thinning of the social net and a global revolution provoked by the spread of information technology. All these tropes lead to this interrogation: Who commands the world? The question sits between some sort of desire for a superpower to exist that could change and organize the state of chaos that is prevailing and the rejection of superpowers in general, at least as they manifest themselves in day-to-day politics. One hears quite a lot about the loss of confidence in political parties and their leaders, in the ability of nations to drive the people they represent to some sort of reassuring future or to build a common ground on which to develop and prosper. These concerns are beginning to be publicly expressed in movements such as Occupy Wall Street. Numerous manifestations in the last year in different parts of the world echo a growing dissatisfaction and desire to reclaim "dignity" as the sensation of loss and powerlessness gains momentum. The concept of a "general strike" is being discussed. A strike in this world context is a

utopia that can be useful in waking up populations and individuals. However, it is some sort of No Manifesto, a negative, opposing stance standing up against a nauseating and paralysing situation. A strike is symptomatic of an ailment, of a blockage; it presupposes that some desires and proposals for some other ways of doing things are not being listened to. It is a live manifesto that enables one to protest against a problematic situation. Most often it takes the form of a collective being, a spontaneous get-together.

In addressing the issue of performativity and ephemerality, as I have been asked to do for this book, I cannot only think of these concepts as they are carried out in the arts at this time. They seem to have become the major tropes of "political life" as we are now experiencing it daily. Process has taken over and is now a dominant factor when one looks at how daily life is being experienced. Objectives, end results, values, rules and regulations are just as present. Nevertheless, these concepts, which structure human life, do not occupy the same position as seemed to be the case just a few decades ago, when institutions and values were more stable and lived out in circumscribed, recognizable contexts. The logos that was behind this way of seeing human life and social existence has taken on a kaleidoscopic form. It is multidimensional, always changing, unpredictable and fluid, giving it a chaotic feel. Learning to live in the chaotic feel is today's challenge.

Performativity is the term that can describe not the end results of a thing or an event (which in turn—or simultaneously—relates to a being in space or in time) but what happens in the process of becoming. This process may or may not lead to a definite form of existence. It is still unstabilized. It can be characterized by a sense of flux, something that is moving and that is hard to "catch". This sensation has to do with the fact that performativity is linked to the exploration of the unknown. By contrast to performance, as the term has been used in recent decades by governments, industry, education, in fact in so many spheres of life, performativity is not an indicator of the way, or the best way, a task is carried out. It is not a measuring device and is not structured as a concept in such a way that it can enable any calculations, evaluation or judgement. Performativity is more of a quest. It questions whatever is there to be questioned, to be experienced. It gives rise to speculation and, in this sense, it is a tool for knowledge, for unearthing the unexpected and

opening up to different potentials and possibilities. This opening up is what is needed in the context of turmoil, which characterizes the post-2000 era. It is a locus for invention and redefinition of the parameters that can lead to a collective being that does not cancel itself out by its immobility or its blockages. This collective being resides in individuals with their characteristic distinctiveness, and it is only in the sharing of individuality (the specific character of that which is distinct, unique) that a common bond, a "commonness" can arise. Bonding develops through the mutual recognition of interests and affinities which reflect one's desires and perspectives for a "better" way of living, stemming out of a sensation of flow, movement, rhythm: an interior "dance".

The performativity that has been characteristic of the Occupy movements is linked to the transience that characterizes performativity. Spontaneous gatherings through the web as much as through formalized associations link the organizing that goes on behind these movements. Here, it is clear that performativity is the other side of ephemerality, as the movement is spontaneous, temporary and contextual. It is bound to fade away as the feeling of urgency motivating it disappears or because it is silenced or repressed by official forces.

Artistic practices carry a good dose of performativity and ephemerality. The current times encourage a cross-investigation of these tropes as they surface strongly in socio-political situations as well as in the arts. Museums have been showing performance (here the word refers to a form or rather, as I call it, an attitude in art) again, after having abandoned it for more than a quarter of a century, and are now promoting consistent performance programmes. Possibly, this has to do with marketing, attracting new audiences and enlarging or keeping up the interest of museum-goers. Nevertheless, the "live" event forcibly brings a feeling of life as it is being experienced. The time factor is important. Time brings with it a sensation that life is being experienced: it brings a *feeling for life*. The body is involved in receiving stimuli and consciousness is gained in the reception of the event that drives performativity. This sense of consciousness leads to empowerment. It puts one's imagination to work. The fact that this experience is to be had in a collective situation increases the sensation of empowerment, of gain rather than loss. In this sense, it counterbalances the ill-feeling of disempowerment

or loss provoked by the anxiety-ridden political and economic situation that we are witnessing and experiencing as common phenomena.

In the last eighteen months or so, I have encountered several instances in the field of art where the tropes of performativity and ephemerality have been noticeably put to work.

Some of these issues were dealt with by choreographer Richard Siegal in *©oPirates* (2010). This piece follows a series of danceworks that Siegal elaborated in several solos and duos, working out the body's territory, its relation to space, time and text. In all instances, the context led to a physical, bodily exploration of being in time and space, of the meaning of being *here*. Possibly, it would seem to be too obvious to say that Siegal, during this period, was exploring what performativity is about, what transience or ephemerality are about. In a sense, these works can be seen in hindsight as being exactly that: philosophical meanderings through performative space. The attitude put forth here consists of searching beneath the skin for what corresponds to what is beyond, or what the great beyond could be, that metaphysical space that is daunting for all humans, as they are endowed with body and mind. Extending his explorative stance beyond the solo pieces he created for himself (with himself), he touched upon the space of the other and investigated that space in a one-to-one fashion in subsequent works.

In *©oPirates*, he not only worked with four dancers but also with participants from the city (Munich) where the piece was rehearsed and brought to life. He worked this out using each participant's distinctiveness in a common world. Bodies, individual knowledge and practices were woven together to form a common stance, a moment of sharing a commonality. Ephemerality was put in the foreground, as the development period that preceded the outcome, the coming out of a common knowledge, had been based on each and everyone's ability to put forward their distinct performative being (in an aesthetics of the gift): a being which exists as it acts, and acts in letting go of the uniqueness of what constitutes the self.

In the end, it is apparent here that performativity and ephemerality lay at the forefront of the *unavowed* community or the *coming* community.[2]

1 See *Higher Powers Command*, after Sigmar Polke, catalogue of an exhibition of the Lhoist Collection, Belgium, 2010. Text by curator Chantal Pontbriand. Polke's work of the same title is from 1968.

2 See Maurice Blanchot, *The Unavowable Community*, translated by Pierre Joris (New York: Station Hill Press, 1988) and Giorgio Agamben, *The Coming Community: Theory Out of Bounds*, translated by Michael Hardt (Minneapolis, MN: University of Minnesota Press, 1993).

CHANTAL PONTBRIAND

Until recently Head of Exhibition Research and Development at Tate Modern, she is living in London and working as an art consultant, critic, and curator. She founded PARACHUTE contemporary art magazine in 1975. Her work is based on the exploration of questions of globalization and artistic heterogeneity. She has curated numerous international contemporary art events: exhibitions, international festivals, and international conferences, mainly in photography, video, performance, dance, and multimedia installation. From 1982 to 2003, she was president and director of the FIND (Festival International de Nouvelle Danse), in Montreal. She recently curated the exhibition *HF|RG [Harun Farocki|Rodney Graham]* at the Jeu de Paume in Paris in 2009, *Higher Powers Command* (after Sigmar Polke, 1968), for the Lhoist Collection in Belgium, and *The Yvonne Rainer Project*, at the BFI Gallery in London, both in 2010. Currently, she is curator of the Paris Photo Live Platform titled "Mutations," and editor of the Platform Book, *Mutations, Perspectives in Photography* (Göttingen: Steidel, 2011). Together with Barbara Formis, Chantal Pontbriand was co-dramaturge of Richard Siegal's piece *©oPirates*.

LOOKING FOR A COOPERATIVE COMBINATORICS
— Hubert Machnik in conversation with Heiner Goebbels

HUBERT MACHNIK Are there starting situations in your cooperative works that are negotiated with an open end, that come into being simply from the desire to work together?

HEINER GOEBBELS Completely free?

HM In the sense that the basic assumptions of the piece develop first in the discussion about it.

HG Yes, it happens all the time. For example, with the performative installation *Stifter's Things* there was at first just the question agreed between the stage designer Klaus Grünberg and me: Is it possible to create a production in which no performer is on stage, i.e. is it possible to structure a concept that creates attention, imagination, tension and relief for the audience, without rooting it in the basic, classical assumptions of theatre, such as the presence and intensity of performers? That was the sole starting question.

As a next step the stage and lighting designer said he would like to work with water, and I wanted to begin with pianos. There was nothing more there to start with. A joint question and these interests, formulated completely independently of each other: pianos and water.

All subsequent developments are then no longer just a form of cooperation between Klaus Grünberg and me, but also a form of cooperation with the whole team and all the elements connected with it. With you in programming the interface, with sound, with video, with light, with the technology, where you basically can't draw the line to the artistic side at all any more. It even becomes a form of cooperation with the material, since I really don't start with the vision of a piece in my head, but rather by posing questions—and I work with what stands in front of me at the end of the development period as an "instrument", in the broadest sense of the word.

Then it flips around, so to speak; then the sounds are there — still without any precise effort on my part. And then out of these sounds I try to "compose" theatre. And, in fact, the very issues that have come up in this process—if you now view *Stifter's Things* as a piece that addresses ecological and ethnological questions — these issues have arisen spontaneously, of their own accord, so to speak. These are really all answers that come out of the material, out of a cooperation with the materials and with the team.

HM But nonetheless, the development process doesn't first start in the rehearsal room but has a prelude, an early notation form, developed before the first set rehearsal at the desk.

HG Yes, but not at the desk. I have formulated interests in advance, excluded things, posed questions, with the end point, for example, being the wish that "I really would like to have a keyboard with which I can link all the theatre media together in a polyphonic way." The musical instruments, the stones, the pipes and metals, the rain, the light etc.

HM The designed space is, after all, also conceived as a transportable space, which, in principle functions the same, or let us say similarly, everywhere, without the particular environment having an influence on the design of the piece itself. How far does the venue change the piece?

HG The piece changes a lot under the changed spatial conditions, because it is very susceptible to the space. And when we play it in a cramped, mediaeval monastery in Avignon, it really is something completely different from the big, wide Armory Drill Hall in New York—and this applies to the audience's associations and imagination as well. Whether on the side stage of an opera house or in the cellar of the Technical University in London—the colour of the space, the acoustics of the space, for example, play a large role here.

We've performed it mostly in black boxes, black rooms, verging on the claustrophobic. Then more of a menacing, frightening mood is evoked, whilst when we perform it in the white, lofty hall of the Hellerau Festival Theatre, it seems more friendly and inviting.

HM Without you intervening in the musical and theatrical material, adapting the light, sound and stage, perhaps changing the dramaturgy?

HG The sound of it changes as well. There are dry spaces where you hear every crackle "like in the woods". And there are spaces that have their own structuring acoustics with a lot of resonance, as in a church or a bunker vault. And that really defines our perception as well.

What's interesting in this cooperation between Klaus Grünberg and me is, however, above all, that the visual stage and the acoustic stage remain relatively separate right to the end. From the approximately fifteen "scenes" into which you could divide the piece, the visual stage is separated from the acoustic stage—or at least not identical with it—in about twelve of them. We see something different from what we hear. That means the original cooperation and independence of the work—not in terms of its radicality as with Cage and Cunningham—keeps on right to the end. And perhaps that's the real power source of my work with Klaus Grünberg, that we don't serve each other—there can be quite a productive friction as well—but rather we can combine the visual with the acoustic again and again, and can also separate them again, in an interplay of making sense and taking it away. Perhaps this starting position of hearing and seeing remains so radically separate, especially in this piece, because there are no communicating bodies. This separation does actually occur in the other pieces as well—when the actor stands with his back to the audience and you can only hear his voice through the microport—even though the communicating body is there. This body, which communicates between hearing and seeing, is not there in *Stifter's Things*.

HM The performance space plays an enormous role for me, too. Setting a piece in very different spaces changes the perception of the composition, the attention to the various aspects. Most recently with Richard Siegal's performance installation *Civic Mimic*, which we've performed up to now in three spaces that could hardly have been more different. From an open, white space in the Hellerau Festival Theatre, via the black box in the Muffatwerk in Munich, to the grand foyer in the Théâtre National de Chaillot in Paris.

HG That's what's nice, that you can travel with pieces and can look at your own work anew and as a stranger again and again. If it is open to it.

HM Open structures play a role in *Civic Mimic* and not only with respect to the perception and the space. I also keep the means of composition open in a certain way when it comes to the choreography and the stage space

HG As improvisation?

HM Interpretation would be more accurate. Not only do I adapt the sound quality to the space at the mixing desk and change the position of the loudspeakers but I also react as a performer to the dancers' performance.

HG You change the musical substance of the piece as well?

HM I wouldn't go so far as to describe it like that. First of all, I work on basic musical structures and then assess how binding they are during the rehearsals. Some survive and are fully composed. In the case of *Civic Mimic*, I also developed a "machine", which enables a directness, a close contact between music and dance. The dance is actually tightly choreographed but the decision as to when something happens is left to the dancers. I wanted to create a similar momentum for me as a performing composer as well.

HG That's really almost the exact opposite of what I'm talking about right now—are you concerned here with an identity of movement and sound?

HM No. Not that. I try to produce a sort of directness, but one which is not descriptive.

HG Which can also be contrapuntal?

HM Yes. I've found that however abstractly the composition and the choreography is constructed, the force of habit is so strong that strangeness, in whatever form, only lasts a short time. So the dance is harmonized with the music and vice versa.

HG Okay, yes.

HM The counterpoint, in the sense you just described it, is already given with the decision on the medium, but also occurs situatively from the experience with the media. I react in detail to the situation in the performance area and the sound development. Also very much in the sense of an emergency, or inherent necessity, which arises from what is going on and expects a reaction and seduces the performer, within the bounds of the composition, into finding unexpected solutions.

HG But you don't want to put them at the mercy of chance?

HM No, chance has a certain pattern, which didn't interest me here, rather the oscillation between event and intent.

HG But you are actually the body who decides that.

HM Yes, I'm the body that decides it, but I don't work with samples, which characteristically have a defined content, but with an underlying composition, which lasts an hour. The keyboard key I press defines the moment in which I make the "tracks" of the composition audible and process them live electronically.

HG And you know what's on the tracks?

HM Oh yes, but I work, so to say, asynchronously through the score. I use a pool of gestures. I denote a movement on the keyboard in time as a gesture. A gesture can occur at different time points in the course of the composition. The tempo, based on what is heard, then decides when fermata are introduced, when the gesture is interrupted and, under certain circumstances, carried over into a new one. The system is based on a composition I wrote while preparing for *Civic Mimic* and it developed into the main creative medium during rehearsals. There are also, of course, some fully composed, synchronous pieces, islands of recognition, as it were. This method gives me the chance to involve myself directly in the course of the meandering choreography, creating a septet instead of six dancers and accompanying music.

HG That means the musical layer retains its independence for the observer, even when its relationship to the choreography builds itself in a different way every evening?

HM Yes, the music has its own individual voice because it also follows its own rules. It doesn't conduct and isn't conducted; it enters a symbiosis on a higher level. This developed during the work together and this cooperation with Richard Siegal and the dancers challenged me to make music which otherwise wouldn't have occurred to me just like that.

Is there something like an improvisation process for you before the composing?

HG While composing, yes—not before composing. With *Stifter's Things* I stood quite alone for about a week in front of the keyboard and the programme you built for me, in the performance space. And like you with the dancers, I reacted to the materials and the space and the possibilities in a way that was quasi-improvisational; I then held on to something and used it maybe in a completely different place. So in this way, in practical terms, the whole musical and technical action went "through my body".

Perhaps even a sort of joint (or organic) breathing arises through this—though that would be maybe too much to say of these machines—but nonetheless a sort of unity of the materials arises somehow.

HM It's interesting that you say that it went through your body. The relationship between sound and body in electronic music is regarded today rather in the sense of an alienation, because the musician is, so to say, no longer connected to the sound production and doesn't get the resonating body to vibrate with a direct playing movement. But the perception and appraisal are for me anything but bodiless and not only, I think, because I also play instruments in a classical way. Dancers and performers don't want to believe this sometimes, probably because of the high level of abstraction that is intrinsic to loudspeakers. But I can only do something reasonable if it's gone through my body too.

HG That distinguishes a composition process like the one we are talking about right now from the big score written by a composer. It does go through the body of his writing fingers but then it really is so overlaid with the desire for complexity and compositional density that it will probably be difficult to still hear the composing body. Which can also be very exciting.

I don't at all want to defend our way of working but somehow it really is a completely different process. Whether I fill a composition on paper with notes and ideas and it's executed at some time, or whether in the end you are closer to the resulting sound with the electronics with which you compose. But perhaps it's also just my inability or even my reluctance to hear the things in my head in advance, before I write them down, because then I would get bored. I find, for example, a studio as an instrument more interesting than writing down something that I imagine. In order to be able to be surprised myself, it's even more interesting for me to work with a mistake that I couldn't have thought up myself and then to use it musically.

And that, by the way, is also something that structures my work with Klaus Grünberg in a similar way: the fact that although we formulate interests—like the water and the piano—we basically don't approach this sort of work with finished visions, but rather "find" the images and sounds and don't "invent" them. And, of course, this way of working, such as we are describing it right now, only works in this sort of laboratory situation. It doesn't work under rehearsal conditions, for which you have to know the result already.

HM Where does that happen for you, apart from in your orchestral works?

HG Exactly! In orchestral works you have to work like that. In theatre productions, by contrast, it's for us a matter of looking for a cooperative combinatorics in order to produce images or sounds that have no explicit reference or symbolism. That's the lowest common denominator for both the visual and the acoustic work: to build images and sounds that have no simple, self-contained meaning, which ideally have no anticipatable structure or proportions.

You open an imaginary space with precisely that space which arises between the images and the sounds, which the spectator always wants to close in a way that is very individual and always different.

HM In your recent theatre works, in which you worked together with musicians, for example with the Mondriaan Quartett, you also use parts of pieces from their repertoire. How flexibly can musicians be worked with in such a context? Is it comparable to the cooperation you previously described but with another medium?

HG Do you mean the scenic work with musicians? Or do you mean the musical ..?

HM Both, working together. How do you deal with the limitations, in the sense of flexibility, that a music ensemble brings with it? How much more do you have to decide before the actual rehearsals? Does something of the directness get lost?

HG When I work with a musical ensemble's existing repertoire, I can investigate the music to see what sort of choreographic and dramatic offerings it makes itself. When, for example—as in *Eraritjaritjaka*—I have a fugue, then I'll place the four string instruments that play this fugue in the four corners of the stage, to make the musical cues visually more transparent as well, to make a fugue quasi-experiential. Other musical structures led instead to placing the string quartet in a line in order to see all the parallel bows as a choreography. Then you get, for example, a "windscreen wiper synchronization" with the violin bows in one of Gavin Bryars' compositions. Then I suddenly see the visualization of a musical figure. That means the analysis of the music choreographs the musicians.

That's exactly the point, when I'm working with music that already exists—and not with my own music—that I am perhaps more able to understand the whole process of making theatre as a musical one. *Stifter's Things* is again a good example of this.

There's a text from Schönberg in which he wishes he could make music with the elements of the stage. In a sense he transposes his musical categories for the theatre elements. He talks about a rhythm of light or a chorus of spotlights. And the keyboard you built me for *Stifter's Things*—where I press F#''' and then the spotlight goes on, or G#''' and the stone starts to move or where it starts to rain with C—that's exactly it. Suddenly, I can think and play the mechanical interaction with the theatre media musically—or contrapuntally deconstruct it in its polyphony.

This can give rise to the sort of images, as for example in *Eraritjaritjaka*, where a deafening string sound from John Oswald stands in contrast to a model house—counterpoints between music and staging, between space and light or text and movement.

The fantasy that Schönberg had with regard to the vagueness or the uncertainty of the musical means of expression was not technically possible at that time. But in the end he wanted to liberate theatre in this way from content as well. You also find statements to this effect from Meyerhold, who pleaded that the theatre director should be above all a musician, even when it's definitely not about music. Theatre, the interaction of the elements, the choreography of light and space and sound and body, is per se a compositional process.

HM As a rule, I'm too involved in the production process to achieve this distance and view. This is the disadvantage of the composer also being a performer. If I work with other music during rehearsal, then it's to experience the difference and to check the rhythm of the whole piece, but not as a shaping element. It's precisely in the theatre and when played over loudspeakers that music quickly develops the character of a playback and thus a reminder effect, comparable to the image of the "bugling stag" on the backdrop, irrespective of the music that can be heard. I'm not saying that there can't be good reasons for it, just that I haven't yet seen any necessity for me. The process you described is naturally quite the opposite of this, if it has anything to do with it all. But back to the flexibility of the media: The processes described often go, as far as I'm concerned, beyond the premiere, i.e. the pieces are continuously changed and further developed in their performance cycle. An advantage, because you can reconsider and change the production all the time, a disadvantage when can't do this on the same scale with a larger apparatus, with musicians. There are, of course, constraints in both constructions. You hand over a piece at the premiere, apart from a few adaptations in the course of the following performances. But in *Eislermaterial*, for example, are there also improvisations, exclusively in the music?

HG Yes, just musical. The space is constructed, the space choreographs the views, naturally. With *Eislermaterial*, by means of the distance I create between the musicians. At times the gap, for example, between the strings is more than ten metres. Then they have to make contact, for God's sake. Then it's not enough that you breathe together, like when you sit together, rather the communication, the arising of a musical intimacy is, as it were, socialized, not privatized.

HM Your last piece with a musician ensemble was *I Went to the House But Did Not Enter* with the Hilliard Ensemble. That was fully composed throughout, right from the beginning?

HG By the dress rehearsals, yes. But developed with them over a two-year process. The Hilliard Ensemble very much appreciated it because they had never before been able to check, change and try the pieces out again with a composer over such a long period of time. So it was not at all like with orchestral music, where the score is simply delivered. We started almost two years before the premiere and I hadn't written a note. We only got at all close to the music relatively slowly.

HM Have you worked together with film makers or visual artists recently?

HG I had an absolutely beautiful cooperation with the video artist Michal Rovner for *Fields of Fire.*

HM What was that about again? I saw a bit of it on television. Were they swarms or liquids?

HG It's oil. Oil in Kazahkstan. She had made a video there of an oil flame that shoots out of the ground and then we worked together for a really long time. I processed a tiny snippet of the sound that this oil flame makes with lots of different programmes and procedures. But the speed of the flow is identical and connects image and sound. Then she, for example on the basis of my sound suggestions, changed the colours of the image, and I, on the basis of the new colours and forms, changed the sound in return. That went back and forth for months—in a very nice, open process.

HM There's a screen or a projection?

HG A projection on a wall—approximately ten metres long and four metres high. The image material is extremely artificial. The starting material in her work is always quasi-documentary and then completely distorted.

HM Yes, that's very much a working method I use myself, too.

HG Always having something real as the basis, so the material isn't synthetic.

HM Yes, origin has something but I often don't know why something interests me. It's not thematically defined but, on occasion, a subject is nonetheless the starting point. Recordings that I've made with a flash recorder, in rehearsals, in cities or simply on my doorstep. I work on it, distort it, leave it alone, until the knowledge of the conditions doesn't play a role any more and it can take on a new role or then again not.

Are there interactive installations that interest you?

HG The set rehearsals. These are the really interactive, first experimental rehearsals. Whether the works are still interactive when they are performed is a question of definition. For example, in *Max Black* the cooperation between actor, sound engineer, sampler player, lighting technician, pyrotechnician and stage technician is incredibly complex, you could even say "interactive", but that's not what you mean. You're asking if something completely different could also develop in one of my performances.

HM In this case it's actually more about cooperation between insiders, where the passive observer doesn't play any direct role. I mean interactivity in the sense of the forming of a sound or image space by a user, who, as an observer, is at the same time actively involved in events. Up to now I still hold this to be a well-meant illusion, since it is mostly only paths of simplification that are trodden—"it has to work"—even if the technology behind it gets more and more complex. But there are some nice exceptions here as well ...

HG I've never done anything like that. Inter-passivity interests me more.

HM Inter-passivity? What does that mean?

HG The possibility of delegating your own activities to external objects ... When, for example, someone sends me a CD to listen to—which happens nearly every day—I sometimes put it on in my workroom but then go into the kitchen and let the space listen to it on its own. Only if I suddenly get called out of the distance from the space when I'm in the kitchen does the recording have a chance ...

HM A tactic that I should note under "involving the spatial conditions". I have a different question: We've spoken a lot about *Stifter's Things*, as an example. You made—and not only with *Stifter's Things*—a transmission into another space, into a pure sound space, like a radio play. What, I mean apart from checking the material for its suitability, what interests you in this and how do you implement it in a new medium? Does it need a different density?

HG No, I think it's rather the other way round. I can abandon the demand for a particular density, which interests me in the performance context, for example if, some time later, after the work has been completed, I listen just to the musical layer—also in the sense of relaxation, which I probably wouldn't allow myself as long as I'm only working acoustically. It's a bit like the difference between a CD and a concert, like when you compare a live "Prince" CD with a studio album, he plays twice as fast on the live CD because the concert needs a different presence. If you put the live CD on at home, the tempo can get on your nerves—that's why you put the studio CD on, because it's more relaxed and reflects the listening situation. I profit from this difference when I leave the visual layer out and suddenly, as for example in *Stifter's Things*, listen to how the ventilator is blowing in the big pipe and think, "Oh, what a great sound." I couldn't enjoy it like that live, because in this scene all hell is let loose with all the exploding bubbles on the water surface.

And it's this freeing yourself from images that interests me here and also leads again and again to surprises. We've already spoken about the difficulties for the musicians in *Eislermaterial* in playing together, in spite of the large gaps between them. And when it was recorded, some of the Ensemble Modern musicians were, to start with, somewhat sceptical about releasing it, because it really is rhythmically wobbly due to these difficulties, and not always together synchronously. But this is precisely the attraction in the scenic performance: if it's completely together, it would be rather flat and boring for the spectator/listener.

And a process of convincing was really necessary, to realize that this is exactly the charm of this recording (and, in the end, even led to a Grammy nomination). That means that through the choreography of the space you achieve a different musical result, which would be impossible to produce in the studio. In other words, in this retrospective dissociation of the acoustic stage from everything that you can see in the performance, there is always the chance of being able to discover a different hearing pleasure.

HEINER GOEBBELS

German composer and director, born in 1952 and living in Frankfurt am Main since 1972. He studied sociology and music, and creates staged concerts, radio works, and compositions for ensemble and for big orchestra. Since the beginning of the nineties he has composed and directed a series of unique music/theater works: *Black on White* (1996), *Max Black* (1998), *Eislermaterial* (1998), *Hashirigaki* (2000), *Landscape with Distant Relatives* (2003), *Eraritjaritjaka* (2004), *Stifter's Things* (2007), *Songs of Wars I Have Seen* (2007), *I Went to the House But Did Not Enter* (2008) and many others.

His work also includes writings, lectures, and CD releases with ECM records. He has received many international record, radio, theater, and music awards, was composer in residence at the Lucerne Festival, member of several academies of arts, honorary fellow at Dartington College of Arts and at the Central School of Speech and Drama, London, fellow at the Institute of Advanced Studies, Berlin (2007/08), and artist in residence at Cornell University, Ithaca USA.
Heiner Goebbels is professor at the Institute for Applied Theatre Studies at the Justus Liebig University Giessen. Since 2006 he has been president of the Theatre Academy of Hesse and is currently artistic director for the International Festival of the Arts RUHRTRIENNALE (2012–14).

HUBERT MACHNIK

Composer and guitarist. He has played in various ensembles and orchestras, in particular "Neue Musik" and was a member of Ensemble Modern from 1981 to 1989. He composes piano and chamber music, music for theater, dance, film and audiovisual installations, computer music, electronic music, and "radio pieces." Concerts world wide; performances in Tokyo, New York, Montreal, Toronto, Sao Paulo, and in many European cities.

Recently: Professorship at the Justus Liebig University Giessen (Computer Music/Multimedia Applications), *Humboldt/Pym-Travelogue and Prospekt\ion* (Lefkada and Thessaloniki, National Theatre of Greece), cooperation with Heiner Goebbels (Geneva, Lausanne, London, Bochum, etc.), The Berlin Philharmonic Orchestra (Education Dept, Berlin/New York), Blindman Saxophone Quartet (Brussels), Deufert & Plischke (Vienna, Graz, Antwerp, Brussels, etc.), Anouk van Dijk Dance Company (Amsterdam, Rotterdam, The Hague, etc.), Richard Siegal (Berlin, Essen, Weimar, Venice, Paris, etc.), Arto Lindsay (Rio de Janeiro), Vollrad Kutscher (Munich, Bern, Celle, etc.) and The Forsythe Company (Frankfurt, Stuttgart, Munich, New York, Columbus, Basel, etc.).

BETWEEN EVENT AND INTENT
— Hubert Machnik

The computer as a universal recording and reproduction machine has been a controversial subject of discussion in different artistic media. Film music is, for example, still widely experienced as a recording of real, played instruments, although here, with the computer's increasing performance capability and storage capacity, virtual instruments and orchestras are increasingly employed. These relationships change with performances in real spaces. Due to the absence of musicians on a dance or theatre stage, the music fed over loudspeakers develops the character of a souvenir. Pina Bausch emphasized this aspect by using recordings from vinyl records with the crackling and hissing of a much played record. The presence of an

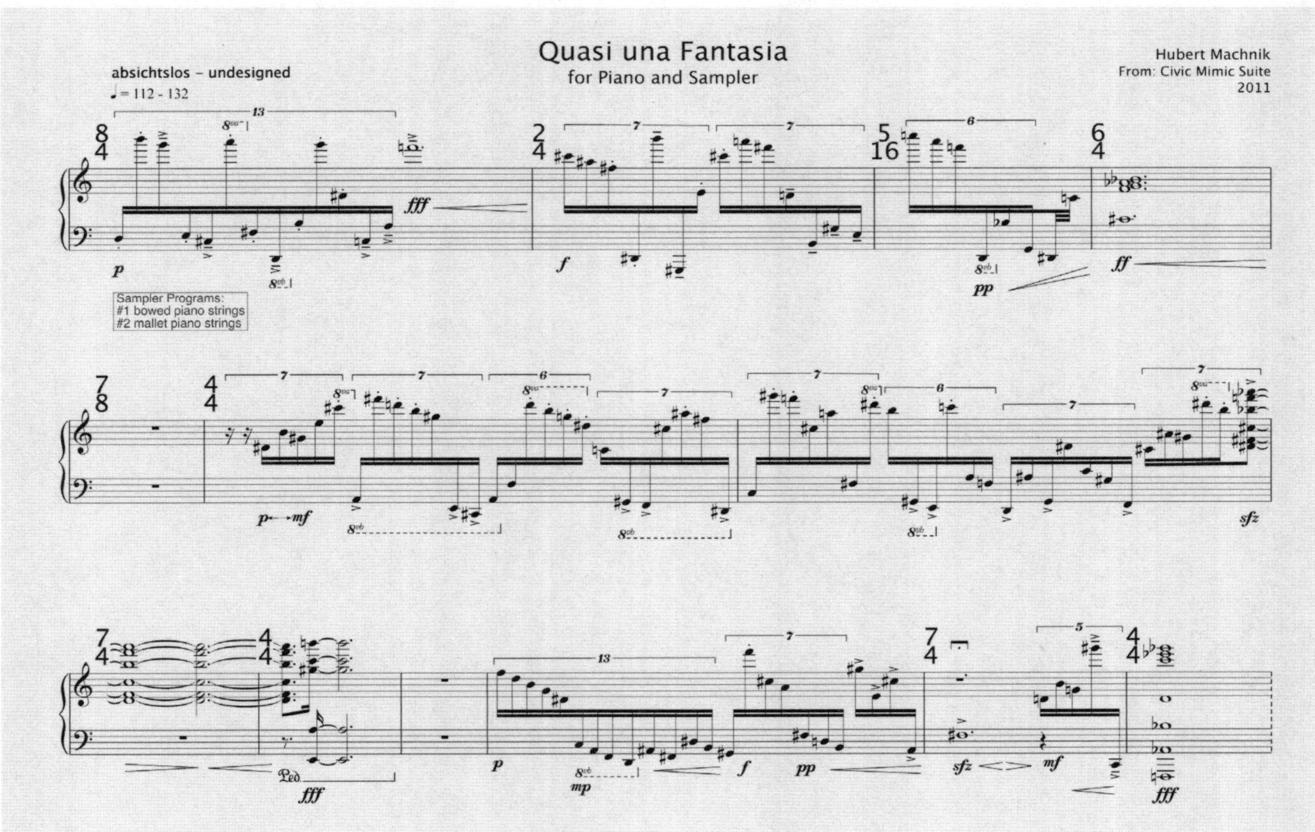

orchestra performing *Le Sacre du Printemps* cannot, despite all the technical improvements in reproduction, be imitated, at least not for those who have heard the work live in the concert hall. The presence of a musician who works with electronic elements appears, in this context, ambiguous. Electronic music has taken over concepts from the repertoire of the classical reproduction media—mixing, playback and fading are operations from the practice of sound engineering. Our notions of a musical instrument are too much connected with the physical production of the sound using strings or keys, and thus with the existence of the performer, for us to be able to understand the manipulation of controls and knobs as playing an instrument. However, because of the musical instrumentalization of the electronic media, that is to say because of their control by means of claviatures and drum pads, the performance of an electronic composition cannot be equated with disembodiment. It is much more that the required gestural repertoire takes on a different form compared to that of conventional instrumental playing. Although this can be represented by means of classical notation, the score does not, however, constitute a general shorthand that denotes a specific sound or tone. The sound arises only out of the programming that underlies it. These programs are an integral component of the composition. With them, completely different structuring elements can be linked with each other using the computer—complex, previously produced phonographic music, that is to say finished compositions, generic elements like sounds, chords and rhythms, generative music programs developed with a programming language, and effects and effect chains, which modify possible input signals. The fact that every detail in the electronic score no longer has to be physically performed as well, makes the artist a listener of the previously produced compositions or structures; he functions between invention and intervention. The intervention doesn't happen by chance, it is rather a function of the invention, similar to the orchestral musician who has to fashion his parts as a function of the performed, and thus also of the heard, work. The corporeal nature of both states, listening and performing, becomes particularly evident here. In contrast to the classical score, which can also be understood by reading, the electronic score can only find its fulfilment in performance. This aspect, the emphasis on the moment and place of the performance, was the focus of my considerations for the music to *Civic Mimic*, a performance installation and collaboration with choreographer and dancer Richard Siegal. Choreography and composition can be regarded as a documentation of movement in the most general sense. As time based art forms, they generate structures which can also be read separately from any thematic references. The gesture, like the movement of the fingers on the claviature in time, stands vis-à-vis the soundscape; the sequence of movements vis-à-vis the representation in a choreography. This division enabled me to work on the two components independently of each other: on the time gestalt, in direct interaction with the dancers during rehearsals and performances, and on the compositional elements in the pre- or post-processing. The choreography for *Civic Mimic* made a repertoire and system of rules available to the dance that, through a chain of decision possibilities plus the involvement of the audience and the spatial conditions, never led to an identical result. The live composing musician is an integral part of these events. He reacts to the developments in the performance area and articulates the underlying composition in a different way with each performance. Thus arose a sixty-minute composition, which up to now comprises twelve layers, as well as an instrument that excavates and processes them. The programming allows access to the layers by means of a master keyboard. Specific keys are assigned to effect chains, which additionally change the time gestalt and the sound. During the performance, the complete composition is replayed. But it remains inaudible, as long as the performer doesn't press a key. The moment at which a key is pressed, as well as the decision as to which key is pressed, determines the auditory result. Thus, metronomically exact tone sequences can be noted, which, with precise reproduction, lead to the same auditory result. If such a tone sequence starts at another time point, it must, so to say, listen to itself, adapt and vary itself, or generally speaking find other interpretive solutions. In *Civic Mimic* the relation between composition, musician and instrument, performance area, choreography and performance is fluid.

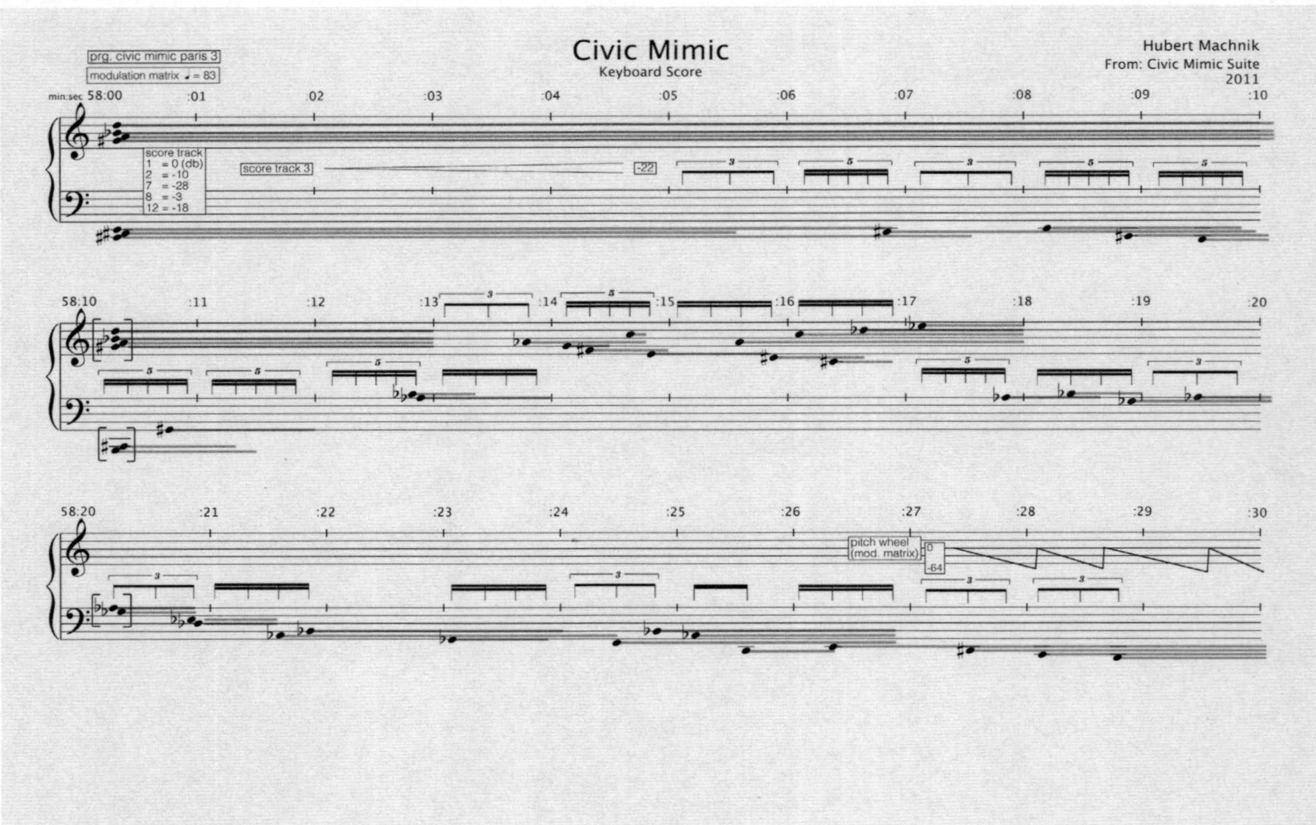

HUBERT MACHNIK

The biography of Hubert Machnik can be found next to page 56.

ORDER FOR FREE

Emergent Improvisation as a System for Composition and Communication

— Susan Sgorbati

A school of fish, a herd of elephants, a flock of birds, a swarm of bees, a brood of hens, a colony of ants, a bevy of beauties, an exaltation of larks (James Lipton)—these are all examples of groups of living things. The phrasing suggests that these living things are collaborating in some way. They are in relationship with each other. Their collective behavior is not without meaning. We can discern order in this seeming chaos of groupings.

A pod of seals, a kindle of kittens, a gam of whales, a wedge of swans, a shoal of bass, a bouquet of pheasants, a gaggle of geese, a parliament of owls (Lipton again)—more groupings whose terms are less known, but easily imagined in motion, shifting the landscape they inhabit, without a leader who maps out their destinations, but capable of creating an essential ensemble through an intricate process of self-organization.

These groupings in motion are an example of a kind of organic structuring that I have named "emergent improvisation." To date, my work in the practice and performance of Emergent Improvisation has focused on improvisation in dance and music ensembles. In this context improvisation is understood to mean the spontaneous creation of integrated sound and movement by performers who are adapting to internal and external stimuli, impulses and interactions. Ordinarily, we think of order and form as externally imposed, composed, or directed. In this case, however, new kinds of order emerge, not because they are preconceived or designed, but because they are the products of dynamic, self-organizing systems operating in open-ended environments.

This phenomenon—the creation of order from a rich array of self-organizing interactions—is found not only in dance and music, but also, as it turns out, in a wide variety of natural settings when a range of initial conditions gives rise to collective behavior that is both different from and more than the sum of its parts. Like certain art forms, evolution, for example, is decidedly improvisational and emergent, as is the brain function that lies at the center of what it is to be human.

Emergent forms appear in complex, interconnected systems, where there is enough order and interaction to create recognizable pattern, but where the form is open-ended enough to continuously bring in new differentiations and integrations that influence and modify the form. It is by way of these interactions that particular pathways for the development of new material are selected.

In linking the creative work of art-making to the emergent processes evident in nature, we find a basis for a rich and textured inquiry into how systems come together, transform, and reassemble to create powerful instruments of communication, meaning, and exchange.

Emergent Improvisation explores the ways in which natural processes underlie artistic expression along with the possibility that art can help illuminate natural processes.

Living things in our environment everywhere are revealing to us the profound depths of structuring processes. Whether it is human anatomical systems, animal migration patterns, insect ensembles, plant morphology, or cellular development, there are hundreds of thousands of forms that have refined themselves over centuries of motion, adapting to their surroundings. *What connects them if there is no pre-defined choreography? Who determines the sequence and the arrangements? Who do they follow? Why do they form patterns? Why are their formations so beautiful?*

Seven years ago, I was fortunate enough to meet two scientists who are masters in their fields. Their visionary thinking greatly influenced how I began to interpret my observations of improvisation ensembles in the dance studio. The first meeting was with Dr. Gerald Edelman in a residency at The Neurosciences Institute in La Jolla, California where he is the director. Dr. Edelman is also the founder of The Neurosciences Research Foundation and chairman of the Department of Neurobiology at the Scripps Research Institute. Dr. Edelman received the Nobel Prize for Medicine in 1972. Our many conversations and my reading his book, *A Universe of Consciousness*, resonated with my own thinking.

Dr. Edelman's work includes a theory of consciousness that is based on neuronal group selection. His theory states that there are two fundamental properties of conscious states: integration and differentiation. My understanding of these properties is that every conscious state contains a unified whole and cannot be broken into individual parts, and, at the same time, each state can be highly differentiated and lead to many different behaviors. These concepts deeply resonated with my observation of the dancers and musicians. The improvisational forms I was observing in the studio were producing coherent patterns that could not be deconstructed to each dancer and musician, and yet produced endless variations. I questioned whether this level of complexity was a further amplification of the conscious state of each dancer and musician.

Another concept of Dr. Edelman's theory that resonated with my work and influenced my thinking was "the remembered present." This concept relates perception to memory. He defines perceptual categorization as "the ability to carve up the world of signals into categories adaptive for a given animal species." The remembered present links the imagined or immediate present experiences with a past history of behavior. Memory is a process linking past to present, actually reconstructing the past into the present. Memory is dynamic, and emergent, not static. This understanding of memory resulted in an improvisational ensemble form called "Memory Form: The Remembered Present."

The second scientist whom I was fortunate to meet is Dr. Stuart Kauffman. I continue to be in collaboration and in ongoing conversations with Stuart, and he is without a doubt, one of the most significant and transformative thinkers of our time. Stuart Kauffman is considered "the father of complexity." He is a founding member of The Santa Fe Institute, the leading center for the emerging sciences of complexity. Dr. Kauffman is a winner of The MacArthur Award, the former director of The Center for Biotechnology and Informatics at the University of Calgary, and is currently the first Macmillan Scholar-in-Residence at The University of Vermont's Complex Systems Center. In his books, *Origins of Order, At Home in the Universe, Investigations*, and *Reinventing the Sacred*, Dr. Kauffman is interested in seeking the construction principles of adaptation, believing that such systems naturally reside on the edge of chaos, what he calls "order for free." Poised between order and chaos, this is a result of a highly tuned selection process. When Stuart visited Bennington College where I teach, he came into my dance studio and inspired me to explore and name The Complex Unison Form with the dancers and musicians. His latest thinking revolves around two conceptual frameworks. One is on the consequences of the unpredictability of Darwinian pre-adaptations (how the squirrel eventually becomes a flying squirrel) and on how the creative process is always pushing us into the unknown, what he calls "the adjacent possible." These concepts are inspiring me to research new improvisational ensemble forms based on multiple perspectives.

Now the Dance Studio has turned into a laboratory for systems thinking. The scientific knowledge of these two great men combined with my own research served as the basis for my understanding of complexity in improvisational ensemble forms. I started to name patterns with the dancers I had been seeing for years. Patterns were interactions that had an understood sequence, design, arrangement, or relationship. They were observable as similar but not always identical units, whereby the boundaries and constraints determined the relationships in time and space. I began to see structures emerging that encompassed those patterns. Structures defined themselves as developmental patterns, relationships of more than one pattern to each other setting up more complex organization with longer time spans. Finally, emergent compositional forms developed out of the continuous practice in patterns and structures of the ensembles of dancers and musicians, as if a kind of evolution had taken place. Emergent forms are frameworks for developmental structures. Just as maple trees are different from oak trees, although they share common characteristics of trunks, branches and leaves, so emergent forms have shared characteristics but unique, essential natures. Over time, ensembles of dancers and musicians build the capacity to identify and repeat recurring patterns of development.

There were three key concepts that emerged in this collaboration and dialogue: self-organization, emergence, and complexity. They were all easily observable by watching the dancers and listening to the musicians.

1) Self-organization, in this context, means the ordering or structuring of people or entities that do not have a director or pre-determined script. The ordering is coming from within the system.

2) Emergence—an outcome or property of self-organization—is the process by which some new structuring/ordering, some new pattern, arises to create another idea, opening up or exposing the potential for something new.

3) Complexity, in this context, is the result of a self-organizing ensemble, creating emergent structures that connect in even more diverse forms. The dancers and musicians are exploring how the many components of a particular system give rise to a collective behavior. Complexity is a structuring at this edge of chaos, where there is enough order to recognize a pattern yet enough openness to be adaptable to new information leading to the creation of a new property or outcome.

This comprehension of structuring principles in the natural world informed my own observations and allowed me to "see" more and literally integrate my perceptions in what I call a more "topological" fashion, meaning that my attention could focus on a local, regional and global level simultaneously. Let me explain:

When an ensemble is composing while improvising, beginners often can only imagine their own movements, maybe in relation to the dancer next to them. In contrast, advanced improvisers, who have been practicing compositional skills for years, can pay attention to their own highly developed physical vocabulary, the dancer next to them, the small ensemble patterns around them, and the global structures in the entire space. This nesting of patterns within structures, and structures within forms, creates complexity.

How does Emergent Improvisation work as a system of composition?

In order for dancers to advance in the practice and performance of Emergent Improvisation, they train in a solo practice and an ensemble practice. An individual needs to have a diverse and original movement vocabulary, an attention to composing on a local, regional, and global ensemble level, an ability to focus on particular patterns, an understanding of spatial relationships, a tracking of the amplification of movement information as it is relayed throughout a space, and a knowledge of compositional development over time while making choices in the present. The goals of a solo practice are to advance in the skills of invention, articulation, attention, versatility, and virtuosity.

In the ensemble practice dancers begin composing with one another. This does not involve a compromise of autonomy or movement material, but includes a sharing of information and an ability to connect with physical and sensory signals. Simple patterns are observed and learned. Dancers learn unison, repetition, referencing, accumulation, framing, nesting, and amplification. Emergent structures then follow. Embedding such structures as main events and choruses, waves and eddies, washes, charges, landscapes, fields, and tableaux, I observed and named several emergent forms such as The Complex Unison Form (named after Kauffman's "order for free") and The Memory Form (named after Edelman's "remembered present"). These forms each have a beginning, development, and ending. There are rules that always repeat themselves, but no two compositions are exactly alike. They each have their own defining characteristics, reflect complexity, and move from transitional spaces into new emergent patterns.

Emergent Improvisation is also a system for communication.

Communication is a process of exchanging meaning with others. The exchange of meaning within a dance ensemble can be through the use of metaphor, narrative, or physical energy—textures, geometries, and spatial patterns—but at its heart it relies on awareness and responsiveness to the choice making of others. In this work we view the dance ensemble as an adaptive, complex system capable of self-organizing structuring processes. The ensemble practice in Emergent Improvisation asks a group of dancers, each with his or her own unique movement history, to commit to collectively selecting patterns in the structural development of a composition. Working in an ensemble in this way requires and encourages the development of specific individual capacities for communication and collective choice making. While many individual capacities contribute to an ensemble's ability to self-organize, several have emerged as central to this work:

Pattern Recognition: This is the ability to observe and signal the organization of relationships as they emerge within the development of a composition.

Negotiation of Roles: This direct interaction is between the dancers. Serving the development of the composition is a priority, and noticing how one's preferences support or detract from the interests of the group composition is an interesting and challenging manifestation of the practice.

Listening: Active listening, amplifying, and supporting the choices of others are all important aspects of attention. This does not mean imitation. What it does mean is an awareness of relational possibilities and shared responsibility for compositional development. Listening can happen through several modalities, including but not limited to aural, visual, and kinesthetic sensations.

Tracking: The capacity for the dancer and musician to simultaneously track at the local, regional, and global levels of the composition enables local interactions to build rich, textured global pattern formations. This collective tracking creates deep connections and investment into an emergent group sensibility. The ability to track the development of the composition and contribute to the collective decisions about the selection and adaptation of patterns is the unfolding of a form.

Attention to Development: This attention to development builds on the capacity to track and is also strengthened by knowledge and awareness of developmental arcs and time-based compositional skills (referencing, retrograding, accumulating, etc.). (Sgorbati, Blocker, Climer)

Most importantly, Emergent Improvisation calls for a balancing of individual impulse and ensemble choice making, with a sense of responsibility to the composition and immediacy in problem solving.

Balancing individual impulse with collective choice making depends on the capacity to simultaneously focus on the particular, track local interactions, and remain aware of emerging global patterns. In this work the dance ensemble is a self-regulating system, requiring feedback loops that enable constant adaptation of patterns in the development of the composition. Feedback is the constant process of initiating and responding that results in the dancers creating enough order to recognize patterns, while at the same time remaining open to the integration of new movement material. (Sgorbati, Blocker, Climer)

The relationship between agency and ensemble is complex within this practice because the compositional development and unfolding of structures is dependent on the collective decision making of an ensemble. Even distinguishing between individual and collective choice making can be difficult in this work, as it is through the emergence of an ensemble consciousness that the compositions develop. Agency and the development of one's solo practice is highly valued in the work, as the contributions of individuals enable ensemble forms to develop with richness and complexity. In many ways agency is strengthened through the process of co-creating, as having the support of others can expand one's perception of range in choice making and development. (Sgorbati, Blocker, Climer)

In developmental patterning, ensemble recognition of one pattern to the next requires ensembles to undergo states of transition. Essential to self-organizing systems is the willingness to work in a mediated space in these transitions, in which the value of co-creation overcomes conflict between agency and ensemble. If the dancers are in conflict during transitional phases and do not form patterns collectively, the system cannot self-organize. In this way, a significant aspect of agency is the decision of an individual to participate in the process of co-creation and collective meaning-making, as it expresses the value of the capacity of an ensemble to develop patterns and exchange meaning in a way that one could not do alone. (Sgorbati, Blocker, Climer)

Ensemble communication is essential to the process of self-organization as it enables the development of an ensemble consciousness from which to compose. These capacities for communication are central to emergent structuring processes, and have implications for contexts outside of the dance ensemble.

I have worked with The Complex Unison Form cross-culturally now several times. First, I worked with a group of South African dancers and American contemporary dancers. The second time I developed work with a group of American contemporary dancers and traditional Chinese folk dancers from Yunnan Province. The third time I worked with a group of traditional concert dancers and musicians from Mongolia, an accomplished dancer from Burkina Faso in western Africa and a group of American contemporary dance students. In all of these contexts, movement styles and vocabularies that were very different merged into a new form. Since we did not speak the same language, we were only able to communicate through the non-verbal language of movement. We each had our own movement vocabulary based on our histories and identity. Retaining our autonomy but sharing this vocabulary transitioned us into a new experience where we were co-creating a new complex movement form together. This form did not represent any one particular group but emerged as a new vocabulary developed by the ensemble in the present moment. This new "complex unison" form happened without a choreographer or director showing us how this new movement vocabulary would emerge. All three experiences were very powerful and immediately created empathy and connection between us. This transformative experience allowed me to identify even further with self-organizing processes in the natural world, as if some larger meaning and purpose was unfolding between us, unspoken, but strong and lasting.

More and more, contemporary composing artists, whether visual, dance, or music, find themselves in this complex, interdependent world, merging their traditions with contemporary styles. African choreographers are making work about dancers in France. Dance students from all over the world study in Senegal and Belgium. Japanese choreographers make dances for West Africans. We need not give up our identity to influence and be influenced by others. We are adapting to new, creative, and interesting relationships and structures. We have the choice to learn from each other and create new global, regional, and local forms or destroy each other, fighting over who should impose their will. We have the potential to create ensembles of empathetic relationships. We are in a process of collective meaning-making, merging our practices to create new forms for a challenging future. I believe this has profound meaning for the way we can experience the diversity of our world and yet maintain our uniqueness. Artists will always be out in front providing a vision for how we can affirm life. If it is true that "order is for free" and that an emergent collective "order" is providing us with meaning and knowledge, then it follows that we can participate in ensemble building to discover it. Maybe then we don't have to spend so much time finding a way to "pay" for it or to ask someone to tell us what it is and how to find it. This order reveals itself in the beauty of the natural world all around us and in the complexity within us. It is this essential connection that we can find with each other and in the patterns that we build together.

* The phrase in the title of this essay, "Order for Free" was first coined by scientist Stuart Kauffman in his book *The Origins of Order* and has been adapted for Emergent Improvisation.

Edelman, Gerald M. *Neural Darwinism: The Theory of Neuronal Group Selection*. New York: Basic Books, 1987.

Edelman, Gerald M. and Tononi, Giulio. *A Universe of Consciousness: How Matter Becomes Imagination*. New York: Basic Books, 2000.

Edelman, Gerald M. *Wider Than the Sky: The Phenomenal Gift of Consciousness*. New Haven: Yale University Press, 2004.

Kauffman, Stuart A. *The Origins of Order: Self-Organization and Selection in Evolution*. New York: Oxford University Press, 1993.

Kauffman, Stuart A. *At Home in the Universe: The Search for the Laws of Self-Organization and Complexity*. New York: Oxford University Press, 1995.

Kauffman, Stuart A. *Investigations*. New York: Oxford University Press, 2000.

Kauffman, Stuart A. *Reinventing The Sacred*. New York: Basic Books, 2008.

Lipton, James. *An Exaltation of Larks*. New York: Viking Press, 1968.

Sgorbati, Susan and students, Marie Blocker and Emily Climer. Conversations at Bennington College, 2011.

SUSAN SGORBATI

Susan Sgorbati has been involved in the field of dance for over thirty years as a choreographer, artistic director, dancer, and master teacher. She is currently on the dance faculty at Bennington College in Vermont, where she has been teaching since 1983. Susan's professional dance work has been presented at various venues in New York City and New England, including Danspace Project at St. Mark's Church, Movement Research at the Judson Church, the Brooklyn Academy of Art, the New York City Improvisation Festival, The Vision Festival, the Improvised and Otherwise Festival, the Jacob's Pillow Dance Festival, Middlebury College, Temple University, and in 2006 a national tour that performed at The Neurosciences Institute, Bennington College, the Flynn Center for the Performing Arts, and the 6th International Conference on Complex Systems, hosted by the New England Complex Systems Institute.

Susan Sgorbati has been seriously investigating improvisation as performance for over twenty years. For the last seven years in collaboration with scientists, she has been exploring the relationship between dance and music improvisation and complex systems. In 2001, Susan began a series of residencies with the Flynn Center of the Performing Arts, conducting workshops and performances within the framework of her new dance research. Known as the *Emergent Improvisation Project (EIP)*, this new performance work reveals the interrelationship between natural, complex systems, and dance and music improvisation, exposing the scientific theories of self-organization, emergence, and complexity. She is currently working on a film with Elliot Caplan called *Convergence: The Emergent Improvisation Film*. Also, this winter 2012 Contact Editions will be publishing her new book on Emergent Improvisation.

ENTANGLED
Performance, Technology and the More Than Human
— Chris Salter

In the mid-2000s, *Theater Heute* featured an article arguing that video cameras and television screens had overrun the German stage as scenographic elements in the productions of young directors. Such technologies robbed the theatre of its most precious resources: the words of playwrights and the bodies of performers. In an age where half of the world communicates through the medium of electrical signals, such pronouncements seem downright silly or technophobic. But this technophobia reflects something deeper in the human psyche—the loss of our anthropocentrically situated universe to things, tools, apparatuses or machines that we have created but that also seem to be beyond our immediate control.

Writing in *Artforum* in 1967, the former Bell Laboratories engineer and founder of E.A.T. (Experiments in Art and Technology) Billy Kluver stated that "it is not a question of what the artist should do, but what he will do with technology." Kluver, of course, was referring to the radical 1967 experiment entitled *9 Evenings: Theater and Engineering* where a battery of engineers from Bell Labs worked for a turbulent period of eighteen months with up and coming New York performance and visual artists such as Deborah Hay, Lucinda Childs, Robert Whitman, Robert Rauschenberg, David Tudor, John Cage and others to create a series of at the time unprecedented, collaborative works of stage art which utilized the technological apparatuses of the military-industrial complex.

But we do not have to cite such important but somewhat forgotten utopian projects to assess the impact of how technology operates on and has endlessly transformed our understanding and experience of what performance praxis is. Indeed, we were already past this debate with the first theatres in fifth century Athens. The collapse of temporary seating platforms in the Agora (the Athenian marketplace), believed to be the location where the first dramatic festivals took place, resulted in the architectural construction of the *theatron*—literally, the place of seeing that separated audience and performer both physically and acoustically from each other—in the Theatre of Dionysus that adorned the hillside of the Acropolis. The *theatron* was both a physical and perceptually demarcated space ordered by technology—a separation of the spectator and performer and mediator of visual/acoustic relations achieved through technical-architectonic means.[1]

1 *Entangled: Technology and the Transformation of Performance* (Cambridge: MIT Press, 2010), page XXII.

In the Western consciousness, *techne*, the word that lies at the root of the term technology, does not imply machines running out of control and eclipsing human nature. Philosopher and musician David Rothenberg describes technology as that which extends human action out into the world. Technology establishes sets of connections between skill (*techne*) and order (*logos*). But forces beyond us are always thwarting this attempt at extension. Citing the writings of the pre-Socratic philosopher Heraclitus, Rothenberg argues that we can never really grasp the *logos*, the order of a world in constant flux and impermanence—in this "account of a world which holds forever, men prove uncomprehending, both before hearing it and after they have heard."[2]

2 David Rothenberg, *Hand's End: Technology and the Limits of Nature* (Berkeley: UC Press, 1993), pages 2–3.

In other words, there is a tension between us humans wanting to order a world that continuously eludes us, slipping from our comprehension and control.

While technology is immanent to the act of "performance", we are also long past the point when the performing arts could claim the word as their own. In our contemporary cultural context, disciplines as diverse (and divergent) as anthropology, gaming, psychology, sociology, art, design or marketing all use the word with abandon. But why this new, almost meteoric rise, given that there were already some substantial "performative turns" in the past, with anthropology and sociology in the 1970s and cultural studies in the 1990s? What does performance imply and what does it promise?

As a concept, "performance" suggests an act or a "doing"—the behaviour of someone or something over time. Time here is the critical element, for the word's original derivation from the old French *parfournir* ("to complete totally, to furnish forth, to carry out thoroughly or to bring to completion"), already implies change—a challenge to a Platonic world of given essences and static states. Indeed, performance—although variously used to articulate anthropological, sociological, cultural and scientific frameworks for late twentieth-century thought—does not only describe what we understand as bodies performing on stage but something that is perhaps more relevant to our contemporary moment.

Beginning in October 2011, my alma mater Stanford University began offering an online class on "Artificial Intelligence", a course in which an unprecedented 136,000 people registered worldwide. The course "introduces students to the basics of Artificial Intelligence, which includes machine learning, probabilistic reasoning, robotics, and natural language processing." Additionally, the instructors, who include Peter Norvig, who is the director of research at Google, "aspire to excite you about the field of AI. Whether you are a seasoned professional, a college student, or a curious high school student—everyone can participate." [3]

3 www.ai-class.com/overview. N.d. Accessed on October 15, 2011.

From a historical perspective, the version of AI that is being taught online radically moves away from an earlier 1950s vision of the science that tried to create computational models of thinking that were termed "general problem solving" approaches — general mathematical abstractions that attempted to describe cognitive processes as purely internal representation in the brain with no reference to an outside environment. The Stanford course, however, focuses on AI as a "perception-action" loop between the "agent" and the environment itself. The agent (which in this case is not a human body but rather a piece of software) perceives the state of the environment through sensors and can affect the state of the environment by way of actuators.

The late computer scientist Mark Weiser wrote,"The most profound technologies are those that disappear. They weave themselves into the fabric of everyday life until they are indistinguishable from it." Weiser was referring to a new computer technology paradigm he labeled "ubiquitous computing" — a vision where computation, enabled through small, low powered devices, could be seamlessly embedded and distributed into the environment around us. The object of computing (i.e. the device of the computer itself) would fade into the background, thus freeing up "users" to focus on what tasks they wanted to accomplish with the computer rather than the computer itself. In essence, with computation being "woven into the fabric of everyday life", physical reality, the environment in which we were situated in, would rapidly become *computationally augmented*. [4]

4 Mark Weiser, "The Computer for the 21st Century." *Scientific American Special Issue on Communications, Computers, and Networks* (September, 1991).

The idea of a world of technologies constituting the environment in which we live and breathe seems again like a science fiction fantasy designed by engineers who view humans as essentially like computing devices. What happens to nature if technology itself is increasingly embedded into the fabric of everyday life? When our very actions and the actions of the environment seem to be determined by a technological feedback loop? To address this quandary we need only turn back to theatre history. As the classicist Rush Rehm wrote in his book *Radical Theater: Greek Tragedy and the Modern World*, the fifth century Theatre of Dionysus (and indeed, all of the Greek theatres of the time) was open to the natural world. Behind the *skene*, the wooden façade and later, building-like structure, which served as a space for the actors to store and change masks and costumes, lay the civic world of Athens and the natural world. In essence, the "scenography" of the theatre was composed of an intertwining of the civic, technical and natural. As the late Hellenistic and Roman periods arrived, however, the *skene* became the more encompassing *scaenae frons*: a stone wall/backdrop that constructed a visual block between the theatre and the world outside.

Rehm argues that the Athenian stage was "deeply grounded" and "cosmic in purview", bringing together the humans and the gods under "exceedingly confident" conditions but what is interesting and necessary from our perspective today is to think of performance from an even more expanded point of view, taking into consideration the acts, the performances of all forms of life—biological, technical, social, planetary. [5]

5 Rush Rehm, *Radical Theater: Greek Tragedy and the Modern World* (London: Duckworth, 2003), pages 21–23.

In *The Mode of Existence of Technical Objects* (1956), the French philosopher of technology Gilbert Simondon declared "culture has become a system of defense designed to safeguard man from technics. This is the result of the assumption that technical objects contain no human reality."[6]

6 Gilbert Simondon, *The Mode of Existence of Technical Objects*. Translated by Ninian Melamphy. Unpublished.

If the stage still seeks to maintain itself as a viable mode of cultural expression, what then could it gain by again looking outwards—to other disciplines and ways of acting in the technical world that we have always inhabited—rather than looking inwards to safeguard itself from the ecologies and networks of the technical-socio-natural world through the sanctity of the human against the nonhuman (animal, plant or machine)?

In many contemporary artistic and design practices (particularly in the technologically inflected arts) there is a marked move away from the performative acts of strictly human bodies and towards an emphasis on environments of techno-scientifically orchestrated things, transient objects and processes. Indeed, many artists and designers (not to mention engineers and natural scientists) are increasingly focused on the performances and acts of these nonhumans. But they are not the only ones. Sociologists, anthropologists, philosophers and cultural theorists are also grappling with our contemporary amalgams of the natural, technical and social, which defy categorization. For over thirty years, the proponents of the field of STS (Science, Technology and Society) have been trying to understand the performances of what Bruno Latour labeled "hybrids"—that is, how the strange and transient objects created in laboratories and studios are constituted, what they do and how they materially operate on the world.

These are not just academic issues that are the purview of philosophers. From the collapse of interdependent global financial markets, the ecological catastrophes of Fukushima or the increasing biopolitical invasions into all facets of social life, such socio-technical monstrosities demonstrate to us the urgency of trying to understand a viewpoint beyond strictly ourselves. If the origin of performance in the West thus attempts to bring together the gods and man, *techne* and nature, the human and the nonhuman, it seems that the urgency now afforded to the stage-based arts is to reclaim the word performance as well as embrace the new concepts brought to it by other fields of knowledge—ones that concern themselves with the performances of all types of life. What are we waiting for?

CHRIS SALTER

PhD, artist, Director of the Hexagram Centre for Research-Creation in Media Arts and Technology at Concordia University (Montreal), and Associate Professor for Computation Arts at Concordia. He collaborated with Peter Sellars and William Forsythe before co-founding the collective Sponge. Salter's performances, installations, research, and publications have been presented at numerous festivals, exhibitions, and conferences around the world. His first book *Entangled: Technology and the Transformation of Performance* (MIT Press) was published in 2010.

A) PERFORMA
Biennial, Think Tank, Museum Without Walls
— RoseLee Goldberg

B) INTERVIEW WITH ROSELEE GOLDBERG
— Dieta Sixt

(A) The PERFORMA[1] biennial, was established to create a highly visible international platform, specialized in a kind of thinking about Performance, acknowledging its historical roots and radical propositions as well as its ongoing effectiveness as a critical reflection on the present and recording its history in appropriate ways. Another purpose was to reignite civic and cultural activism, to bestow community once more on a congregation of artists from disparate disciplines whose sensibilities, imagination, and creative drive need points of connection to survive and flourish.

The material of the 1960s and 1970s was indicative of a period when art-making was an investigative pursuit and when one of its goals was to produce experiences for the maker as well as the viewer. Connecting the dots between the loft and discount store and gathering places where the artists all met provided a map of Lower Manhattan that was a modern urbanist's dream. It showed a "walkable city" of streets animated with people day and night en route to buildings that would be set in motion by unexpected events and happenings. It showed a city grid, unscrambled by a diversity of jobs, ways of living, class, and ethnicity, and an urban landscape that could sustain a high level of street energy around the clock.

This patchwork of intersecting lives and purposes, made possible by cheap rent and an unassuming aesthetic that was the opposite of the stifling consumerism, brand-name marketing, and escalation of real estate values over the decades that followed, encouraged creativity among artists and audiences alike. It was this atmosphere that the PERFORMA biennial would seek to resuscitate; linking venues, people, and places, it would use New York City's rich Performance history, and the cutting-edge metropolitanism it fostered, as springboard and inspiration.

PERFORMA 05
INAUGURAL PERFORMA BIENNIAL

The first biennial opened on November 3, 2005 and was to last three weeks; it began with the promise to curate a collection of work, both historical and contemporary, that despite being presented within a curatorial context, would remain unstable and problematic. As curators of the first visual art Performance biennial, we sought to show and tell, give and ask, prod and produce material that, above all, surprised even those of us who thought we knew it well. Only this much we may anticipate about Performance by artists: expect the unexpected. Only one overarching instruction was given – focus on visual artists, for the inaugural biennial must establish an understanding of the central role of Performance in shaping the history of twentieth-century art, and also show its ongoing importance in the opening years of the twenty-first.

The idea of asking visual artists, some of whom might not have contemplated Performance previously, to create multimedia productions that would take place over an extended period of time and that would connect with audiences through the presence of live performers, grew from the proliferation of film and video installations in galleries and museums over the past decade. Rather than the ten or fifteen minutes typical of these projections, our commissioned

DIETA SIXT The three books, PERFORMA 2005, PERFORMA 2007, and PERFORMA 2009 are more than a documentation; they help the reader to understand the importance of individual artistic works chosen by the PERFORMA team in relation to a larger historical trend.

(B)

ROSELEE GOLDBERG I guess I am deep down an art historian. I want to be able to investigate the ideas of the artist and I approach curating as I do writing my books. You are trying to tell a very live story, you are trying to explain the history of Performance and it is really about the way artists think, sort of like pulling back and seeing the big picture and discovering where ideas begin—and often ideas begin in an action, in a live kind of presentation where an idea gets sparked. Historically this has been the case over and over again.

If you look at a Malevich painting, everybody thinks his first white paintings were done in 1917, but in fact the first one was done in 1913 in the Performance *Victory over the Sun*. My feeling is that some of the most radical events start out that way. They begin as a kind of action. So how do we describe this art historically, how do we articulate the process of the artist's thinking? The artist is really at the heart of this and trying to get as close as possible to where creativity begins. The history is very clear for me in many ways: the Futurists, the Russian Constructivists ... I am really taking apart what these different histories mean to us, rethinking them.

DS When you initiate the curatorial process of the biennials, when you start off with your team, where is it that you begin?

RLG I think where I really start is with the commissions, because the whole idea of PERFORMA was to commission new work for the twenty-first century. As far as the commissions are concerned, it is really about desire.

It is almost too personal to describe what desire is. It is like when you fall in love with somebody or you see somebody walking down the street and your breath is taken away. What is that emotion? How do you describe that? For me, each of the commissions has come about because of seeing an artist working, thinking. And obviously it is work that involves a sort of narrative or some way where the body is in it.

Similarly with Jesper Just. He had only made eight- or ten-minute videos and I saw just the first few minutes of one of his first videos before I invited him to do something. Because I was really getting this desire to have those personae, those personalities, that were inside the television box, inside the screen, step out of the screen. And to be there in a visceral connection with that player.

It is really about desire. I think that's what we all look for in art. I mean, why do we walk around every day looking endlessly at art. We are looking for these experiences that are so elevating in terms of the intellect and our emotions and your visceral responses and colors and sounds, and everything that art does for us. So I look for work that I feel will make people feel something. That you would feel on many, many levels. And it is really that personal.

(A)

> Performances would run longer, giving the possibility to fully absorb the occasion of a contained spectacle without interruption, to capture the artist's unique take on the belief systems and aesthetics of our times.

PERFORMA 05 opened with Jesper Just's opera *True Love is Yet to Come,* which he himself would see for the first time fully executed only twenty-four hours before opening night, and which proved the PERFORMA proposition that nudging the Performance genre in entirely new and unexpected directions would indeed bear fruit and result in remarkable and original productions.

> The whole idea of PERFORMA, two years after the first PERFORMA Biennial took place, is to take the very best of that earlier New York energy and use it to charge the contemporary scene. That period is critical for me. When we went to a Performance in those days, something really stayed with us, our perceptions were altered. We can do this again. Life in New York can be artist-driven; it doesn't have to be institutional. The community in the 1970s was much smaller, the economics were different, and everyone lived within walking distance of one another. In conversation with the artists of that time–Laurie Anderson and Eric Bogosian, for instance–they talk about how they knew their audience would be made up of other artists from the downtown scene, which had to affect their ideas. I also look to other periods when the art and intelligentsia communities were wrapped up in one another, like the 1920s in Paris or Berlin, for example, and think, "Wow, look what they were doing then."

The idea for PERFORMA is to commission works that provoke the future, to reignite the energy from the past, and shake things up in the present. My hope with our Commissions is that by spending more time with a work, the ideas and sensibilities of the artist will be planted on one's psyche forever.

PERFORMA insists on a community of action and of the imagination. By connecting people, places, and ideas, it calls for a new kind of humanism to enhance the lives we lead.

> What I'm seeing in New York is that Performance has actually been dormant for a while and artists were waiting for this opportunity to do work that they can call Performance again. Maybe Performance never stopped, but people used other words, like intervention, action, Happenings, or even "live event." The terminology does change and indeed the medium keeps changing. Because of the nature of the art market right now–its dominance and sophistication–we are at a point where people want Performance, they want an outlet, they want to be liberated.

In addition to this unusually orchestrated, totally immersive series of events, PERFORMA also made space for focused discussion. *Not for Sale,* a series of ongoing panels begun one year earlier in preparation for the biennial, was a symposium at New York University on the subject of writing about Performance and the multiple disciplines covered by the term. Also addressing multiple issues surrounding Performance, its relationship to art institutions, to the marketplace, and to the world

(B)

PERFORMA moved forward slowly: the first year (2005) we had three commissions; the second year (2007) I think we were up to ten and we thought that is a nice number and we would stay there; but suddenly at the third round (2009) we had twelve and this year (2011) I think we are up to sixteen. So many projects are commissions or works that we develop with the artists. And it is really again about providing profound experiences for the viewer. I think we spent an enormous amount of time thinking about the experience of the audience. I mean, somebody recently asked me: "What is the difference curating a biennial and Performance as opposed to objects?" I said, you know, my feeling is that you experience what happens when you leave your house and what happens on the way to the Performance, during the Performance and after the Performance. Can we find a great café where everybody can go and argue and discuss this piece that hopefully moved them or meant something to them? I feel that that experience of the viewer is just optimum—finding the optimum way to feel the piece, to find spaces that were actually bringing up the flavors of the work in the most exquisite way. These are things we think about and talk about all day.

DS My suggestion is that we focus on PERFORMA 11 at the moment. It is uppermost in your mind: thinking about it, establishing surprises for the public. Perhaps you would like to give some sense of the continuity for PERFORMA 11?

RLG That's a good point to just quickly throw in here. I think PERFORMA is very unusual as a biennial, because we do have the continuity of the team and a sort of intellectual continuity. I think so many biennials have a new curator every two years and there's a whole new statement and mutual rethink. It starts from scratch every time. I think that it is actually very exciting that we can build on these concepts that started right at the very beginning.

I was seeing a lot of work that was just being repeated from earlier years and I had the idea to think about this extraordinary history, to revaluate that history, to bring it to life in really remarkable ways and to provoke the future by inviting artists. Many of them haven't done Performance before. To really think about the issues that are involved in Performance. What happens when you step out, what happens when you have that live presence of the artists and the live presence of people basically in communication with one another.

Another part of the structure of PERFORMA that I realized in retrospect was what I call the historical anchors. PERFORMA 09, of course, was Futurism, but that only comes once every hundred years. But there are other anchors: this idea of how much work we have to do to really investigate that early material and to think about it and how to make it lively and relevant for a young generation today. Why should they pay attention to Futurism, why should they pay attention to Russian Constructivism? It is rather to look at those early periods and take an example from the way art was positioned in those environments.

(A) of ideas, the discussion further reinforced the necessity of PERFORMA's stated mission: to expose the full impact on art history of live Performance by artists over the past century.

> I am often asked whether each PERFORMA biennial has a theme or direction, and the answer is yes, but you wouldn't necessarily know it. The first biennial in 2005 had a plan that was not immediately obvious: it set out to right a wrong, showing that Performance by visual artists was not the sideshow portrayed by art historians in the narrative of twentieth-century art, but rather a main event.

Ideas take form in actions, and actions by visual artists actively shaped the art of the twentieth century. Artists who made Performance were at the forefront of the front—the avant avant-garde—and they frequently broke more radically and thoroughly with prevalent art styles and concepts than others.

PERFORMA 05 succeeded in getting this message across. It showed live Performances by more than ninety artists that took place in a variety of venues—on a flat-bed truck, in a burlesque club, on an island in the Hudson River, in galleries, a museum, or over the radio—and triggered enthusiastic interest perhaps unprecedented in the history of artists' Performance.

PERFORMA 07
EVERYWHERE AND ALL AT ONCE
AN ANTHOLOGY OF WRITINGS

PERFORMA 07 built on this momentum, opening the door to other disciplines (dance for example), expanding the Commissions' roster (from two to ten artists), and inviting more than sixty venues and over twenty curators to join our plan of action for invigorating the city with a cultural activism not seen in decades.

In 2009 our *Dance After Choreography* program explored new directions in dance from the point of view of the visual arts. It comprised a series of Performances, film screenings, and discussions that pointed to an important chapter in the story of American art, in which dancers and artists, musicians and filmmakers worked in tandem, especially in the 1960s and 1970s in New York, and in particular at the Judson Church, were the Judson Dance Theater (1962–64) was born. Pioneering figure Yvonne Rainer provided a starting point from which to examine the work of a generation of highly intelligent and history-minded French choreographers emerging in the 1990s, who were profoundly influenced by Rainer thirty years on. That her ideas crossed the Atlantic and reappeared as incisive and polemical dance, executed in an entirely different language, prompted the invitation to two choreographers at the forefront of that movement, Jérôme Bel and Xavier Le Roy to participate in PERFORMA 07. Their reimagining of Rainer and the Judson generation's parsing of dance into its basic elements—body parts, walking, talking, standing still—and their combination of these fundamentals with the particularities of a deeply French education, specifically

(B)

The historical subject matter for PERFORMA 11 is Russian Constructivism. There were a lot of issues involved: it was about the fact that in the early 1920s, at the height of idealism—the Utopian idealism of the early days of the Russian dream of communism—artists had an extraordinarily important role. They were the transmitters of information, essentially in an illiterate population. There was this extraordinary group of artists. They came back to Russia after many of them had been living in Paris in their early teens with this sense of vision about what the artist could actually do, to translate the new society for this larger population. Hence, you had agitprop trains and boats and something called "the living newspaper," which the Russian Contructivists were also very intrigued by. This idea that you can, on a daily basis, articulate communism, make it available again using different artistic methods.

That was one of the issues I really wanted to think about. The notion of the artists having a role in society. A serious role in translating the best ideals of a political dream.

DS Right, but it is not only all these ideas of expanded spectatorship. There is an aspect in your own personal view of things and that is being in the position to be so generous—generous to the artists that are chosen, that you don't just look at ten minutes of the Performance, but you are able to give that artist thirty minutes to deliver the message or to deliver a new aesthetic experience. How does this generosity tie in with your being a historian?

RLG That's a wonderful way to put it. Thank you. I do feel profoundly this need to spend time with the artist and with the artist's work. I think stopping time was almost one of my mantras for a while with the idea of PERFORMA. I think of the last wonderful *documenta*, or the Venice Biennale, feeling with the big mega-productions that I am almost exhausted before we get there. But did you really spend time with the work? How much time did you spend? How much were you really able to absorb of that work? So for me, stopping time, really immersing yourself in the artist's ideas coming away from it—hopefully that work stays in your body for a long time so that it is part of your blood stream. That is again the experience that I wish to create.

So the generosity has to do with the sense of total admiration and belief in the artist's imagination. If one can really somehow profoundly let it into one's psyche in a direct way—that is the kind of relationship that I want to develop. So for each of the works it is not even thirty minutes or three months: the conversation might go on for a long time. And sometimes I plant the seed and sort of hope we will be talking about doing performances a year from now, two years from now, to allow somebody to really think about these issues. So it is really my desire to have that full experience when I see an artwork in the sense that one doesn't get enough time with so much of the work we see.

(A)

deconstructivist methodologies, had by 2007 reentered American choreographic vocabulary, coming full circle. Bel and Le Roy, along with Boris Charmatz, whose films were included in *Dance After Choreography*, reignited the tenets of Rainer's radical manifesto-like statement of 1964: "No to spectacle, no to virtuosity, no to transformations and magic and make-believe." In a post-Pina Bausch, dance-as-theater world, they used Rainer's purist concepts as brickbats against the spectacle of European dance drama.

Rainer herself went further back in time, considering what it meant to be radical in 1913 in Paris, when composer Igor Stravinsky and choreographer Vaslav Nijinsky joined forces to produce the riot-inducing *The Rite of Spring*. In her ingenious "restoration" of an opening night long ago Rainer explored not only a seminal work that had changed dance and music history at the start of the twentieth century, but also the ways in which her own far-reaching positions about dance had been folded into that history. Intended to explore the interests of a new generation of dancers, looking at the visual arts as a mirror for their choreographic ideas, and a growing number of visual artists who include professional dancers in their live performances, *Dance After Choreography* cross-pollinated audiences as much as it revived the conversation across disciplines that had been so critical to the art of the 1970s.

Site was essential to each PERFORMA project. Venues were selected for the way in which they extended the aesthetic and conceptual sensibilities of the material, allowing its full "flavor" to seep into the surrounding space and envelop viewers. PERFORMA Commissions were chosen for an inherent theatricality in the work as well as for an innate sense of time and timing that suggested an enormous potential on the part of the artist for working live. Isaac Julien and Russell Maliphant's *Cast No Shadow*, comprising three film installations with live dancers and presented on the stage of an eight-hundred-seat house, allowed viewers to watch Julien's ideas unfold from beginning to end. Live production was both a culmination of, and a departure from, ideas and values expressed in the commissioned artist's primary media. Given that many of them had never created live works before, their daring was considerable—and illuminating—leading to exploratory rethinking of their bodies of work. Translating from one medium to another, moving beyond styles and practices close at hand, and exploring unchartered territory characterized many of the PERFORMA Commissions. Such a description could also apply retroactively to Allan Kaprow's revolutionary *18 Happenings in 6 Parts*, which was originally presented in 1959 in New York and reconstructed during PERFORMA 07.

A concrete illustration of Kaprow's move, as he described it, from being an "action painter" to being an "action artist," *18 Happenings* could be seen as a way of prying out the shapes, colors, and forms of abstract painting to viscerally experience these relationships "in the world." Kaprow's *Happenings* were a sort of guided, step-by-step procedure designed to encourage the viewer to experience perceptual changes in the environment. Restaging *18 Happenings* made this abundantly clear. Performers and members of the audience

DS You are developing a curriculum for the next PERFORMA, but it is again a continuum. I like that idea. It is all about time, isn't it?

RLG Yes, that's right.

DS With all these PERFORMAs you have been actually developing a network, not just nationally but also internationally. You mentioned before your task is that of "planting a seed." So the thoughts that have been actually repeated and developed, and further developed with each new PERFORMA biennial, are now being planted, not just in other cities but other countries too. How does that dovetail with your perspective on cultural history?

RLG It is such a good question again. From day one we have been international, which is very exciting—that a young organization can start out that way. So from the start, our very first commissions were Francis Alys, Jesper Just, artists who are coming from very different places. In terms of planting a seed, I remember Isaac Julien actually coming. When I did the first commission with Shirin Neshat in 2001, which is exactly 10 years ago, Isaac was there. I saw him at the Performance and I said to him: "Isaac, you are next. You are the person I want to work with next to develop a live piece." So the idea for that piece was planted in 2001—I didn't even have the idea for PERFORMA then.

DS That came in 2004.

RLG Exactly. So the moment I had the idea for PERFORMA, I actually went to Isaac first and I said: "Isaac, you know, I am ready to go. What about you?"

DS "It's your turn."

RLG The idea was to do it for 05 and then Isaac's project just got bigger and bigger and more beautiful, and we both—kind of on the same day—looked at each other and said: "Let's not rush this, let's do this in 07. You've still got part two to do!" He was telling me about going to Africa and how this whole piece connected. So the beauty of it was we were able to say, "No one is pushing us, there is no deadline—let's do this in 07." And by the time we got to 07, it was this totally magnificent, major, major work in three parts on an opera house stage in collaboration with Sadler's Wells. If we had done it earlier, it would have been more rushed and more limited in scope.

And even yesterday I was talking with a choreographer, someone whose work I am very, very interested in. He has worked with us in the past and I said—you know, it was really just planting a seed—I said, "Have you ever thought of doing a work that is specifically about New York?" And then we started to talk about the way people move around the city, what it looks like in terms of choreography, what it says about the body.

Or with Francesco Vezzoli, for example. I said to him way back, again when I started PERFORMA, "Francesco, anytime you are ready, just let me know." He had never done Performance before and that is another exciting peak point. And he then came to me and said, "RoseLee, I got this great idea," and the big smile on his face described it. He said it was the Pirandello play and explained how it

(A)

followed detailed directions and profuse notes written for the original event; they were told where to sit and when to move from one partitioned space to the next, when to applaud and when to remain silent. Thus each person attending the contemporary event had first-hand experience of what is not always clear from reading about Kaprow's work—that each of his *Happenings*, despite the casualness implied by the word "happening," was in fact precisely scripted and pre-determined. They also discovered the significance of reenactments of earlier Performance art as a way of refreshing history and seeing it anew.

Providing a context for examining the long history of Performance has been PERFORMA's mission from the start. Without context, the fullness of this rich material remains hidden from public view, insufficiently scrutinized in the broader cultural sphere and therefore incomprehensible to most for being utterly unfamiliar. PERFORMA was established precisely to fulfill this role: a museum without walls, it frames the discipline, providing references, comparisons, and yardsticks for artists and viewers both, to understand the full extent and relevance of this history. It is a hub for connecting the many international players in the field—an ever-growing community of academics engaged in critical dissertations, art departments in colleges and universities dedicated to Performance art theory and practice, Performance art curators and conservators within contemporary art museums, and artists from around the globe. A specialized staff is engaged in research and development, publishing new criticism and writing, and building an archive and photographic documentation with the expertise that comes from concentration.

PERFORMA 09
BACK TO FUTURISM

Each PERFORMA biennial, since the first in 2005, has extended the range and relevance of live Performance art. Performance actions, so experimental and paradoxical from the Futurists onward, forged entirely new ideas about what might constitute art, sometimes resulting in art objects and artifacts that were also three-dimensional installations, installations that were also durational events, and events that took place on street corners, in parking lots, on rooftops, or in far-off landscapes. In other words, many of the artistic high points of the past 100 years prove that Performance art by visual artists is central, not peripheral, to the history of art as we know it. With PERFORMA 09 there was no question where our starting point would be: back to Futurism. It was clear to me that the 20th century began with a series of radical propositions by the Futurists that would shift the very idea of art, transporting it from the museum and academy walls to the street and variety theater, from the painted canvas to the spoken word, from the written page to the airwaves, and from the pedestal of the sculpture studio to live bodies engaged in performed actions of all kinds. Indeed, the first Futurist manifesto of 1909, and the seventeen manifestos that followed over almost two decades, left no art of modern life untouched; probing and provoking, inventing and challenging, they

(B)

was going to happen and what he wanted to do. He wanted to do it in the Guggenheim and I said, "We're on, let's go!" "But I want you to know I am only gonna do one Performance in my life and that is for you and for PERFORMA," and he said this categorically. But, of course, he discovered so much that he could do in a live Performance—the layering of information, the layering of media, the impact—that you simply can't get in a static artwork. It just conveys so much information compared to a painting, embroidery, or a photograph. So I think this whole part of the relationship is absolutely fascinating. And how each person describes what that process has done to their work subsequently.

And something else about the continuity. These artists will always work with us. It is not like, "Oh, you were in the biennial of 07, so you can't come back for five years." There is a platform—those people will be able to work with us always. And in fact we tour a lot in the world too, to get back to your question about getting international. From the very beginning it has been international, because we are all trying to understand this international world that we are living in. This vast sort of global extension.

This enormous amount of Performance is almost the mode of choice for so many artists, because it allows them to express their ideas and gives them access to a much larger public; because people can respond, because it is live and it gives them access to the international community. So I think we are looking at Performance as being the medium of the twenty-first century global culture—it is through Performance that some of the most radical, most profound ideas are shown.

DS And do you see a specific aesthetic in Performance?

RLG There are many different aesthetics and that is the beauty of it. Because they are artists, you know, that is what is so profound too, the fact that you are looking at the handwriting of the artist in such different ways—how they approach Performance. Some appear, some do not appear in their own works. Some like to create a dinner party for you to eat their concept in a way. Tino Seghal does not appear, does not even allow photos. In each instance, the work, the variety is extraordinary.

DS Reflecting on your thought, that the twenty-first century is the century of Performance, then maybe the twenty-first century is the "performative turn?"

RLG I agree, though I am never quite comfortable with the word "performative." But in fact, we are on the same track. I would go so far to say that, in fact, the twentieth century was already *that*, but we never acknowledged it. Which is why I had to create PERFORMA, because I wrote all the same things thirty years ago. The same story was being told that I told in my original book. I think the twentieth century was already essentially driven by Performance. People didn't know where to put this material. But if you think about it and go through year after year, you are looking at work that was so profoundly altered by live work, by action, by activities. The whole notion of the artist's activism that begins with, let's say, the Futurists

(A)

proposed and projected new ways to eat, sleep, fly, dance, and dream. We covered the city with banquets, exhibitions, street parades, noise concerts, sleep-ins, film screenings, and Performances, exercising a vision of urban connectedness that took history as inspiration.

Such compact illumination of the creative realities of the city that never sleeps provided context and framing for the remarkable PERFORMA Commissions, numbering twelve, each with a proposition for a futurism all its own and each providing us with utterly original ways to view our fast-paced world. PERFORMA attempted to stop time for a moment by devoting three weeks to reassess and rethink both how we experience art, and how we know and record it. These biennial centerpieces included an opening-night moving feast, a cell-phone parade, a talk show/sitcom, a mysterious journey through the Lower East Side, and a musical spectacle based on high-school yearbook photos. PERFORMA works closely with each artist from start to finish, from development and production through final presentation at the biennial, including international touring following the New York premiere.

The Futurist banquet officially introduced the Futurist theme for PERFORMA 09, taking the hundredth anniversary on February 20, 2009 as an opportunity to fulfill PERFORMA's mission of bringing history to life in the most original and inspiring ways. "We must invent new foods that induce happiness and optimism and multiply infinitely the joy of living," Marinetti declared in the introduction of his *Cucina Futurista* (1932). An exhibition was created, conceived as a living exhibition, to grow exponentially as it travels from venue to venue over the coming years—*100 Years*, covering each year since 1909, when the Futurists published their "Futurist Manifesto" and launched the Futurist movement with its demands for an art of action and intervention, up to 2009, the time when PERFORMA celebrated the 100th anniversary of Futurism. Functioning as an archive of easily reproducible material, the exhibition was also a history of the style and manner of documentation itself, and of the technology used to produce it. With additional live programs, seminars, and screenings organized each week during its four-month run at P.S. 1 in New York, and a two-week Performance festival accompanying the show when it was presented at The Garage Center in Moscow in June 2010, *100 Years*, which continues to tour, is an important container for a history of ephemeral art, and an exciting new model for ways to make that history palpable, and live, for new generations of viewers.

"In the 19th century, with the invention of the machine, Noise was born," wrote Luigi Russolo in his famous 1913 manifesto "The Art of Noises." The exploration of noise as a phenomenon unto itself was one of the Futurists' most radical propositions, one that PERFORMA 09 fully embraced. Aside from reconstructing the iconic *intonarumori*, or "noise intoner," the biennial also presented a festival of noise music, a radio program, sound installations, band concerts, and an opera singer under hypnosis.

The scant cinematic output of the Futurists was put to impressive use in PERFORMA 09's film programs, which included moving image work by Tacita Dean, paying tribute to the process and aesthetic of choreographer Merce Cunningham. *Craneway Event* is a poignant study of a community, and an intimate window onto Cunningham's working process.

The Futurists' obsession with "simultaneity"—the layering of many different ideas, sounds, actions, or images in a single moment—is nowhere more evident than in multimedia Performance, which has the capacity to combine live Performance, imagery, light, and sound in ways that provoke and inspire. From William Kentridge's autobiographical monologue, with its coinciding representations of the artist himself, to Joan Jonas's intricate collage of Performance, video, drawing, and text, the multimedia events in PERFORMA 09 provided rich views into many worlds.

The goal of PERFORMA's opening night is to set the stage for a biennial that will palpably shift the mood of New York City's cultural life, and to declare the begin-

(B)

and then just explodes all over Europe, and in Japan, in Russia—the idea of the action, activism, people walking up and down the Kurfürstendamm in the 1920s. This notion of crossing disciplines, of the coming together of the multidisciplines, was profoundly twentieth century. It just wasn't being talked about then. Everyone says, "Oh, it is multidisciplinary," but look at the surrealists, look at all the exhibitions they had, look at Hannah Höch—these amazing exhibitions that were done that were all about activity and hanging things from the roof. Max Ernst making an exhibition with wire and string, and you had to walk through different spaces and participate and interact. This has been there for a very long time.

DS Yes, that's true.

RLG To me the twentieth century was already driven by this and, I think, the twenty-first too—because of this global conversation. Because the fact is that the center is in the main centers of commerce, Paris, New York, London, and Berlin—major centers of culture and art hubs where culture is consumed and also critiqued and positioned.

DS If Performance is not only a hub, if it is access, isn't it also a political agenda?

RLG It is definitely a political agenda. If you look at countries like South Africa, where it is about citizenship, it is a sense of being a citizen of a country and having a consciousness to articulate that citizenship. When you do a painting, it is very difficult to say this is my culture, these are my issues—that drive my thinking, that I am obsessed with. So I think two things: firstly I think that, in the twenty-first century, Performance is *the* medium in a very broad, but also highly articulated way, because it provides these doors and windows into this sort of central "keeping house" in the art world; and secondly I think that Performance is the new art history.

PERFORMA has had this profound impact where people who never touch the history of Performance are suddenly writing about it. I am having people finally understanding that it is a way in, and it is the center to fill all the gaps and finally talk about this material. So you are getting writers and young art historians coming to me from all kinds of different areas of art history or contemporary art studies and suddenly discovering Trisha Brown and wanting to understand Yvonne Rainer. And they wouldn't touch that before—that was dance, they didn't know about it.

DS There is one last point that I want to touch on, because it is related to this venture, because it will be an essay in a book. And the books that you have published so far related to PERFORMA are actually very important for your network. Perhaps you want to just comment on that, how the documentation is actually part of the PERFORMA idea and biennial?

RLG Absolutely, and this is again probably something that I thought and talked a lot about. In fact, in my introduction to my big book on Performance in the 1960s, I do indeed talk about the role of the photograph and documentation and you might just want to remind yourself,

> ning of a three-week immersion in the imagination of visual artists. It is a night in which to fully submit to the fact that art gives significance to our daily lives, not only to satiate our desires for aesthetic and visceral pleasures, but also as a means to express the complex humanism that shapes our consciousness. Jennifer Rubell created an event that accomplished all of the above. Startling in its scale, interactive demands, and visual metaphors, her Performance installation took place on three vast floors of a building on Twenty-Second Street in Manhattan.

The elements of the evening followed the order of a typical gala reception—"cocktails," "dinner," and "dessert"—but Rubell entirely upended these conventions. Also arranged in three parts, her *Creation*, inspired by the first chapter of Genesis, provided surprises every step of the way. "The project as a whole serves many functions," noted Rubell. "As a commentary on the artisanal, the original, the unique and the appropriated; as an exploration of ways to engage art history through a medium (food) virtually absent from it; as a catalyst for a working interaction between viewers and objects, and viewers and each other; as a meal; and as a questioning of the boundary between art and all that exists to support it."

Ideas of radical urbanism, the festival as a think-tank, and Performance activating an entire city were all central to PERFORMA 09, which launched PERFORMA's first ever architecture program. Centered around the PERFORMA Hub, a Performance and gathering space that seemed to magnetically draw people to its multi-use interior, whether in New York or Santiago to which it later toured, PERFORMA's architecture and urban activism program enlisted participants to design posters, make their own pasta, among other activities, all of which emphasized the importance of individual action in a collective environment.

The basic idea of the PERFORMA Hub, designed by Berlin- and London-based architectural practice nOffice, was conceived as a space where you constantly form new relations, a space that is always being made and remade while you use it. It was designed for travel as a self-contained PERFORMA module that would adapt to new venues according to the demands of different environments. There were strong visual lines from the front doorway into the space, and onto the street.

> The design seemed to come from a conceptual place, but it also had a sensorial richness to it. And a rhythm. People could roam through the space and feel like it was almost a part of their body. I tell everyone who comes in here, it's not a bookstore, it's not a café—it's a place for ideas. The PERFORMA Hub was the starting point each day for a series of conversations that would provide a reading of both past and present, a veritable "how to" of bringing history to life.

Architecture, and its many communities, was an important new addition to the PERFORMA compendium of ideas. With the "Storefront for Art and Architecture," PERFORMA presented a ten-day gathering of purposeful architects, academics, and urban scholars in a polemical cross-fire of ideas and ideals. In sync with PERFORMA 09's focus on New York City itself—with commissioned projects exploring architecture, design, urban planning, and public space—*Not for Sale: Ideal Performance Space* brought six New York-based architects and designers together to discuss their own projects. Artist and architect Didier Faustino called for architecture that would materialize on the fringes of the city or in vacant lots.

(B)

because ... the problem being, as I am always being told, one reason why Performance is so difficult is because it is ephemeral and, you know, you can't see it if you didn't see it!

So, a couple of answers: The first is, I wasn't in the Battle of Waterloo, I wasn't at the barricades of the French Revolution. It doesn't make those moments in history any less relevant. We do not always have pictures of the things that really change the world. So this notion about art—because you can't see it, because you weren't there—really doesn't hold. The second thing is that with most art we see, we don't see the "real thing." We think we do, but we don't. We see illustrations the size of postage stamps in a book or large illustrations in the book. We see thirty-foot high projections in a hall. There is actually very little relation to what you feel, to what you actually see in real life. We don't see it as the "real thing." So that is critical. If you flip through any book on Performance, the images that come out of this material are like no other—nobody else can dream up these kinds of images that we see in looking through endless files of Performance documentation. These are visual artists who make extraordinary images.

We art historians learn to "read" a piece iconographically. If you look at the little lizard in the left hand corner in a fourteenth or fifteenth century Flemish painting, it tells you something. If you look at documentation, it is an extraordinary history of Performance itself. We learn to read the pictures and I think people have to give up trying to think, "Oh, this is just a photograph." It is a hugely important photograph and, if anything, it is like in childhood—how much about childhood do we know except that we know something about it through the photographs. So the photograph is a wealth of information. Documentation is, therefore, hugely important. As far as the books are concerned, there are so many stories to tell in working with these artists. It is so critical that we reveal history as it is occurring and I think, in some ways, I write the books for the art historians thirty years from now.

DS This is quite the task as I see it for the PERFORMA books, because they make everything that happened, even if you weren't there, come alive. And therefore it is the art history of the next few generations.

RLG Literally, I was thinking that, as a young art historian, I spent all my time looking for documents that didn't exist, about Schlemmer or whoever, trying to run into the smallest corner to find that material. So I am providing that material, so people can really get as close as possible. And, you know, the questions I would want to ask Picabia: What was it like to present a Performance in Paris in the 1930s? I try to create these interviews so that somebody who is sitting in Japan or Korea will be able to read that material and get an understanding of what the artist was thinking about when they made that piece. So for me it has to answer a lot of these questions. The book is another medium that tells you all kinds of other things that you cannot get, no matter how much you stare at a film or a video documentation of a work. So it is all the elements coming together.

(A)

PERFORMA EXPANDS ITS NETWORK THROUGH THE MEDIA

The PERFORMA biennial is the most visible feature of this museum without walls. For three weeks, every other year, it fans out across the city, linking dozens of venues and their various constituents, a crowd of curators, and some hundred artists. A sum of many parts, this entirely new kind of biennial draws on the experience and knowledge of many intellects to bring together a greatly varied program of works large-scale and small, of short duration or long, of bold and seductive or discreet and obscure sensibilities. Interfacing directly with the city, its streets, buildings, public spaces, and cultural venues, the PERFORMA biennial functions as a dynamic form of urban activism, providing places for people to gather, to engage, react, and explore.

Other noteworthy initiatives in the realm of various media included PERFORMA TV, inaugurated in 2007, which is an Internet-based video broadcast and commissioning program that provides a live, open, and public platform for the artists and organizers of the biennial. During PERFORMA 09, the PERFORMA website provided three million visitors with a front-row seat to exclusive biennial content, and spread PERFORMA 09 around the world almost instantaneously. It now forms the basis of PERFORMA's permanent media channel. Listeners can tune in to hear artist interviews and experiments in sound and radio on AIR (Art International Radio), PERFORMA's official radio partner.

While PERFORMA the organization methodically reveals the significance of a long-hidden history and keeps a measure of its many developments, charting questions about preservation, restoration, and even acquisition by museums and collectors, the PERFORMA biennial is a "think-tank," a vibrantly reflexive collaborative organism that responds to the continuously shifting demand of live and provocative material. It could be said, in the words of artist Robert Rauschenberg, to take place in the gap between art and life.

1 PERFORMA, a non-profit multidisciplinary arts organization founded in 2004 by RoseLee Goldberg, is dedicated to exploring the critical role of live Performance in the history of twentieth century art and to encouraging new directions in Performance for the twenty-first century.

(B)

DS How do you perceive the future of 2011 and the biennials to follow? What are you looking forward to? What is your wish for them?

RLG I am very excited, by the way, about PERFORMA 13 (2013). To me it is the excitement of what it takes to understand culture as it is unfolding right now and to build in the knowledge of history that we have, and trying to imagine where we are going in the future. This is a daily rethinking ... even the structure of PERFORMA.

This year we added the school. We were given an old school in Soho, which is an old elementary school. It is a landmark building, a beautiful Victorian, red brick building; it is three floors of classrooms. And the day I walked in there I wanted to cry, because I looked at these classrooms and said, "I want to teach in these classrooms." They are such perfectly shaped rooms, they are just made for you to pay attention. So we have developed a whole program: we are calling it the PERFORMA Institute and it is really bringing together the whole intellectual environment that I have created with PERFORMA from the very start. So the school is this entire new dimension. Last year we added the Hub, the PERFORMA Hub.

DS And invited the architects ...

RLG Yes. So this year we are going even further. We now have a school, which was a dream. It will be this real sensual hub in an even larger environment. So that is new. And for 2013 I am already looking at so many different ways of approaching the kind of intellectual framework. Again these themes are really research themes, which we use to explore all these different relationships. So one of the themes of this year—we have three themes—one is Russian Constructivism and the second is Fluxus. And then we have a whole ... the theme was "language translation and misinformation," because I wanted to talk about the difference between theater and live Performance, the different brain cells we have when we think in the art world—different from the ones we think with in the theater world. Because the world is changing every minute, we will respond to what those next changes are. The excitement about PERFORMA is that we are not working within any historical constructs, so we can respond in the most flexible ways. We will be in a lot of different parts of the world. We already took the PERFORMA Hub to Santiago last year. Witte de With will be the first major European consortium member we have as of 2012.

DS Marvelous, and what a good way to end!

ROSELEE GOLDBERG

Founding director and curator of PERFORMA, a non-profit arts organization which launched the first and only live Visual Art Performance Biennial in the United States, is a renowned art historian, critic, and curator. Goldberg pioneered the study of Performance art with her seminal book, *Performance Art: From Futurism to the Present,* first published in 1979 and the key text for teaching Performance throughout the world; it was published in thirteen languages in its fourth edition. She has written and produced three publications that document the PERFORMA biennials.

DIETA SIXT

The biography of Dieta Sixt can be found on page 8.